T0375408

Writing Success Through Poetry

Writing Success Through Poetry

Create a Writers' Workshop in Your Classroom

Susan L. Lipson

Routledge
Taylor & Francis Group

NEW YORK AND LONDON

First published 2006 by Prufrock Press Inc.

Published 2021 by Routledge
605 Third Avenue, New York, NY 10017
2 Park Square, Milton Park, Abingdon, Oxon OX14 4RN

Routledge is an imprint of the Taylor & Francis Group, an informa business

Copyright © 2006 Susan L. Lipson

All rights reserved. No part of this book may be reprinted or reproduced or utilised
in any form or by any electronic, mechanical, or other means, now known or
hereafter invented, including photocopying and recording, or in any information
storage or retrieval system, without permission in writing from the publishers.

Notice:
Product or corporate names may be trademarks or registered trademarks and are
used only for identification and explanation without intent to infringe.

Library of Congress Cataloging-in-Publication Data

Lipson, S. L. (Susan L.), 1961–

 Writing success through poetry : create a writers' workshop in your
classroom / by Susan L. Lipson.
   p. cm.
 Includes bibliographical references and index.
  ISBN 1-59363-183-9 (pbk. : alk. paper)
  1. Poetry—Study and teaching (Elementary) 2. Poetry—Study and
teaching (Secondary) 3. Creative writing (Elementary education)
4. Creative writing (Secondary education) 5. Poetry—Authorship
—Study and teaching.   I. Title.
LB1576.L5518 2006
808.1'071—dc22

                                                2006003303

ISBN 13: 978-1-59363-183-3 (pbk)

Graphic Production by Kim Worley
Cover Design by Marjorie Parker

Table of Contents

Preface

I wrote this book for both teachers and students, to inspire awe for words and writing. Memorable, meaningful, powerful word choices evolve from memorable, meaningful, powerful lessons. Poetry, which is founded precisely upon such word choices, offers the perfect vehicle to prompt excellence in all forms of writing. Too often, many teachers avoid teaching poetry, even if they themselves are fans. Many educators have never studied poetry in depth, and thus have a limited appreciation for its inherent potential as a tool for teaching writing in any genre. As Charles-Pierre Baudelaire wrote: "Always be a poet, even in prose."

Many teachers may consider poetry "too abstract," "too deep for my students," "too limited in terms of structure," or "not something I'm really comfortable or familiar with." I have heard these very comments from teachers before I have used poetry prompts to conduct workshops in their classrooms as a visiting author/teacher. After hearing the young writers share their work aloud, these teachers expressed surprised delight about their own students' capabilities in responding to poetry prompts.

Writing Success Through Poetry aims to dispel misconceptions about teaching with poetry and to elevate the art of poetry itself in the eyes of students and teachers. The prompts and exercises in this book offer a user-friendly style of guidance, especially structured to meet the many levels and needs of students, while still allowing for the teacher's own creativity in the lesson's application. Both teachers and students will find:

- an immediately usable collection of lessons;
- an array of poetry representing various styles and themes;
- practical, pointed questions supplied to facilitate Socratic-style explorations of literary concepts;
- extensions of exercises to add depth and learning opportunities;

- clearly explained writing exercises that highlight concepts from each poem;
- clear and practical guidelines for running a successful workshop-style, process-oriented program;
- methods to instill writing students with a mental checklist for self-evaluation and future reference; and
- a profound respect for the power of poetic writing in every genre.

In elevating poetry itself, this program will boost the appreciation of individual word power. The exercises elicit experimentation with words in any kind of writing—not only in the creation of poetry. Although one reader might write his or her own collection of outstanding poetry in response to this book of prompts, another might produce a myriad of prose writings that showcase the author's skills in nonfiction (analysis of literature), personal experiences captured in prose, fictitious dialogues, or short stories. Thus, poetry serves as the launching pad for students as they dive into the depths of their own literary skills.

Furthermore, *Writing Success Through Poetry* meets the following national standards put forth by the National Council of Teachers of English (NCTE), available on their Web site (see http://www. ncte.org for the full list of standards):

- Students apply a wide range of strategies to comprehend, interpret, evaluate, and appreciate texts. They draw on their prior experience, their interactions with other readers and writers, their knowledge of word meaning and of other texts, their word identification strategies, and their understanding of textual features (e.g., sound-letter correspondence, sentence structure, context, graphics).
- Students adjust their use of spoken, written, and visual language (e.g., conventions, style, vocabulary) to communicate effectively with a variety of audiences and for different purposes.
- Students employ a wide range of strategies as they write and use different writing process elements appropriately to communicate with different audiences for a variety of purposes.
- Students apply knowledge of language structure, language conventions (e.g., spelling and punctuation), media techniques, figurative language, and genre to create, critique, and discuss print and non-print texts.
- Students participate as knowledgeable, reflective, creative, and critical members of a variety of literacy communities.
- Students use spoken, written, and visual language to accomplish their own purposes (e.g., for learning, enjoyment, persuasion, and the exchange of information).

Introduction

Teachers, as well as parents who homeschool, can use *Writing Success Through Poetry* as part of a language arts/writing curriculum. Motivated, independent young writers who seek enrichment outside of school can also use this book. The exercises challenge students, but, because they are narrowly focused on skills development within the context of short written pieces, these exercises do not overwhelm the young writers.

If you are a teacher who plans on using this book as a manual for writing instruction, please note that the lessons offered comprise a variety of prompts, requiring no specific order of completion and catering to a variety of skill levels and interests. Each lesson features a poem followed by a list of thought-provoking discussion questions that range from simple analysis of word choices to in-depth thematic exploration. You may pick lessons that you deem appropriate or most potentially inspiring for your students. You can also enhance your use of the poetry prompts by combining them, whenever possible, with other related prompts (see pp. 25–27 for additional prompt ideas you can develop), such as:

- pictures of people, landscapes, or objects for descriptive writing;
- printed advertisements that use literary techniques to make consumers remember specific phrases or believe in a certain product's worth;
- telephone books for finding character names;
- famous quotations to illustrate with concrete examples;
- found objects or pieces of art;
- single verbs to practice showing (instead of telling about) an action; and
- songs to inspire writing via music, lyrics, or both.

Whether used alone or in conjunction with other tangible prompts, I have found that the writing elicited by poetry-based prompts often exceeds all others in terms of depth.

Please note that I highly recommend the writing workshop format (described below) for a process-oriented approach to each of the lessons. I cringe at the thought of a teacher assigning one of these lessons, only to have students turn in the first drafts of the works they create in return for a letter grade, some spelling and punctuation corrections, and a couple words of praise.

The Workshop Format

The workshop format entails the following steps:

1. *Prompt*: Read the poem aloud, slowly and dramatically, or have a capable student do so. (This should take no more than 1 minute.)

2. *Discussion Questions*: As a group, read aloud and discuss the questions posed after each poem. Emphasize that these questions may solicit different positions or viewpoints, rather than definite right or wrong answers, and students will need to support their responses with evidence. (The length of time will depend on the poem and depth of analysis by the group.)

3. *Exercises*: Have students complete the exercise(s) as directed after each poem. The extension lessons may not apply to all students, but certainly will help with lag time for slower writers by keeping the faster writers busy and challenged while waiting. Of course, you may decide to have students complete all of the suggested extension lessons, as well. (Approximately 15–25 minutes of silent writing time for each exercise, depending on the size of class, skill levels, and the depth of the lesson.)

4. *Share Work Aloud*: Collect samples to be read aloud, either by you or by student volunteers. To retain anonymity, fold down the corner on which the author's name appears before handing it to another reader. Some students may choose to read their own work, but only ask them to do so if they volunteer. Some writers prefer to remain anonymous; others gladly accept the applause—something I incite—from the audience after each reading. After reading a work aloud and then leading the applause, I always ask: "Would the author of that piece care to identify him- or herself?" (This will require up to 1 minute per piece.)

5. *Comment/Critique Time*: Before the public sharing and critiquing begins, provide feedback guidelines:

  - Emphasize that critiques begin with a specific compliment (students should include "I liked its . . ." with a "because . . .").
  - Remind students that the reasons why they liked a piece can include, among others, the way the author uses description, action, and dialogue; the mood or power of the narrative voice; the depth of character development; the use of vivid, "showing" words, rather than vague, "telling" ones; the structure and flow of the work; and the plot itself. A list of reasons may be written on the board as examples before opening the floor to comments.
  - Invite students to offer a way to make the work even better, if they can, or to pose a question to make the writer clarify some unclear point.

  Limit critiques to three comments per piece if possible. (Approximately 3–4 minutes required per piece.)

  Teacher Modeling: To enrich the meaningful quality of student comments, I often model appropriate feedback myself by asking leading questions, such as "Now, how could the writer improve this piece by replacing one 'blah' verb in that second line with a more vivid one?" Until students get used to the workshop format, such leading questions from the teacher might be necessary to elicit meaningful responses. Require each writer to take notes about comments he or she receives to use in revising the piece. Also, advise the other writers who await their critiques to note any comments that might pertain to their own work. (Modeling time will no longer be necessary after two or three workshops, but allow up to 2 extra minutes per piece at first.)

6. *Peer Editing*: After three or four public workshops, once the students are accustomed to giving and receiving constructive criticism, divide the class into small editorial groups, or pairs, providing each peer editing team with editorial checklists (such as the one in Appendix A) to guide their revision process. The peer editors trade their work and collect comments from each other, then revise their work, and meet again to repeat the process. The students thus turn in true final drafts, thoughtfully crafted, and edited by students, who learn as much from editing others as they do from revising their own work.

  Following the initial peer editing sessions of first drafts, collect the peer editors' comments in response to the Appendix A checklist, along with the first drafts. This method will eliminate the need for the teacher to write copious comments on each paper; a mere "I agree with your editor, and would also like to add _____" or "I disagree with your editor about _____, but agree about _____" will suffice for the first drafts. I recommend at least two revisions before students present a final typed (or very neatly handwritten) copy. Comments about the second revision should include the apparent improvements in the work.

7. *Revision*: Revising makes an appropriate homework assignment, as an extension of classwork. Send home with students the Editing Checklist in Appendix A, so that well-meaning, but product-oriented parents can see how to guide writers into an educational process of revision, as opposed to simply telling them what to change.

8. *Share Revised Drafts Aloud*: It is nice to periodically take 10 minutes out of class time, whether from a public writing workshop or from peer editing time, to read a few revised drafts aloud and solicit public applause (or Beat-style finger-snapping—kids love it!) from their classmates. Showcasing the process of, and progress in, writing motivates students more than any pep talks from a teacher.

9. *Return Proofread Drafts*: Try to hand these drafts back within a day or two, if possible.

10. *Submit Typed Final Draft and Self-Evaluation Notes*: Once students have received their proofread copies, have them type the final draft as homework. Students should turn in the finished work along with the first draft and self-evaluation notes written in response to the Editing Checklist in Appendix A.

11. *Grading*: The finished works will receive rubric scores (see Writing Rubric in Appendix B), but those scores will be based on progress, not on the final product alone. Comparing the first draft to the final version, the teacher will use a 1–6 rubric scale to evaluate the work in terms of the progress (e.g., moving from a 2 to a 5 would give the student a progress score of 3). A progress score could then affect the ultimate letter grade: For example, a progress score of 2–3 would allow the teacher to raise the student's ultimate letter grade by a half-step, from a B to a B+. A progress score of 4–5 could bring up a work by one full-letter grade. You need not provide any rubric score or grade until this final stage, when you can compare the first drafts with the final works. Along with writing letter grades or rubric scores on students' papers,

you should write at least one specific compliment and one specific remark of advice regarding the student author's development of techniques, style, or ideas. In this way, growth, not the grade, becomes the focus.

The workshop format requires flexibility and patience. The objective of this entire program is to create analytical readers who can translate their critical abilities into their own writing and appreciate the power of the written word.

Students may act reluctant to participate in the workshop at first, especially shy students, but I have yet to find the student who decided to remain anonymous during public readings of his or her work for more than three sessions. They all inevitably learn to enjoy the praise from their peers, to value constructive criticism, and to welcome the chance to spend the necessary amount of time on a work, rather than rush to turn in a piece that does not fill them with pride. Students appreciate having not only the time to revise and create their best possible work, but also the implied confidence of their teachers, who, by allowing more time for revision, show their belief in the students' capability for growth as a writer.

As an introduction to your first writing lesson from this book, please present each student with a copy of Appendix C, "Basic Rules for Writing," and the student handout page, "Writing With D.A.D. and M.O.M.: Student Guide to the Three-Step Writing Process" (see p. 31). Both of these references should be read aloud and discussed. Students can keep them in the front of their writing folders or notebooks for easy reference.

Please consider the writing exercises that follow as evolutionary lessons to create works-in-progress, which will lead to finished pieces only after a revision . . . or two, or three. Taking the time to review second or third drafts with students may produce fewer pieces of writing to send home to parents, but the quality of writing will prove inversely proportional to the quantity produced. As a writer who happens to be a teacher, too, I emphasize *revision* as the most important part of learning to write well. No real writer ever published a first draft; no one escapes some editing in trying to get words into print. Every writer, no matter what skill level, needs editors—and I don't mean proofreaders, who just correct final draft items such as misspellings and grammatical and punctuation errors. Editors evaluate content and form—matters of substance.

Many teachers dread grading writing papers and may avoid assigning additional writing assignments beyond what the district or school requires. Dread no more! The exercises in this book will require mainly short works, fewer than two pages long, which highlight specific skills and techniques. The focus on quality, not quantity, makes life easier for both teachers and students. Plus, students assist in the editing process via the writing workshop format, which will turn you and your students into editors by virtue of the mere public exchange of ideas. Furthermore, the self-evaluation process guided by the Editing Checklist in Appendix A furthers the independent growth of each writer, and allows the writing instruction to focus on developing the *traits* of strong writing (see Appendix D) via easily remembered new techniques.

Many students have been misled into believing that the grades applied to written works matter more than both the learning derived from the process and the establishment of one's own personal best standards in writing. You and I must combat this belief and enable our students to understand writing as a process, not a product. Reflect on this: If I, as a writer, were to create my works based only on what others expect or demand from me, I would not truly be *communicating*, only fashioning words to serve others; not creating, but reiterating; not sighing with pride upon completion of a written work, but rather, with relief to be finished. Thus, if I, as a teacher of writing, do not lead my students into careful examination of the words they choose and the reasons they choose them, I fail to assist the communication process. Teachers like us must respond to the words students write with provocative questions and with suggestions for more concise and powerful means of expression. This response must occur before any final drafts are due.

In addition to allowing ample time for students to complete multiple drafts, we must model the type of writing we seek by writing the very assignments we give to our students. Too often students flail about blindly in completing essay assignments given with only vague instructions and lists of sometimes overwhelming quantifiable requirements. My teaching experience has shown that students learn best via modeling and subsequent emulation of their instructor's work; just as the Suzuki method of musical instruction has shown through its continual success, accompaniment by the teacher during instruction enables students to feel like part of an artistic *process*—the making of music—rather than making them focus on missed notes or squeaky string sounds. Suzuki students learn via emulation while playing along with the instructor—a learning process that leads to independent, joyful performances.

In focusing on the process, rather than solely on the product, during writing instruction, we teachers serve as muses—to inspire, enlighten, and guide. In sum, we must practice more questioning (that good old Socratic method) and less judging. We must pose questions that produce detailed and/or profound answers. Then we can guide and enrich revisions by asking, "So, is this what you were hoping to convey?" We need to ask what happened between points *A* and *C*, not simply deduct points for a lack of *B*. We should annotate, not simply grade papers, and offer clear sample essays, not simply clever writing prompts. We can honor communication itself by showing young writers that their words matter enough to elicit our thoughtful reactions and sound recommendations for continued improvement.

How to Justify a Process-Oriented Writing Program in a Product-Oriented System

Some teachers, administrators, or parents may question this approach, which could indeed yield fewer total written works than other programs, in which the number of pages and thickness of student writing files mean more than the quality of the words within them. "Why does my child seem to be writing the same thing over and over again?" a parent might ask. "Why can't he move on to something new already?"

We could respond to such comments something along the lines of this: "If I were his piano teacher, would you ask me why he must play the same piece over and over? Would you want him to move on to a new piece before he could play his current one with pride?" If the parent were familiar with, and appreciative of, music study, that reply might convince him or her of the value of a process-oriented approach to writing.

A more concretely credible justification for this program can be found in Appendix D, which shows how the techniques that form the basis of instruction in this book fit into the highly acclaimed, widely used 6+1 Trait® Writing model, which now seems to be setting the standards for writing instruction throughout the United States. After years of research, the educational team that developed the 6+1 Trait® model has contributed a trait-based perspective on writing that focuses on the writer's growth process. Thus, sound research has proved the importance and necessity of skills-based, process-oriented writing lessons, as presented in this book.

The Power of Poetry: Tools for Any Kind of Writing

All writers owe readers an answer to the question, "So, why should I spend my valuable time reading your words?" Keeping the reader's interest takes practice. A poem requires control from a writer, who must pay attention to rhythm, verse structures, rhyme (sometimes), and emotional impact. Poetry thus represents every quality that good writing should provide, and it demands that writers create words that move across the page not like unruly puppies, going off every which way, but like well-trained dogs, heeling and stopping smoothly, showing careful restraint. Writing poetry is one of the best disciplines to practice making precise word choices. For that reason, I teach poetry writing to all of my students as part of their general writing instruction. The study of poetry provides the basis for all writing techniques.

This book offers poems from my own collection as the prompts to explore many different writing tools and styles, applicable to *any* kind of writing. I have selected poems that display a variety of styles and themes that also address specific techniques with which students can experiment.

The Poetry Prompts and Literary Elements/Techniques

There are a number of important literary elements and techniques that are used in poetry. The box on p. 9 presents an overview of these terms, which are discussed in more detail below.

Some of these poems present simple *imagery*—literal and sensually rich descriptions that capture an image like videotape capturing a memory. In such poetry, the poet need not have intended to add any deeper, hidden meanings (not consciously, anyway). The sole intention is to share something beautiful or poignant. For example, consider the poem "Majesty":

> ### Majesty
>
> Towering, twisted, old tree:
> the sun casts new life
> upon your dry, gray limbs,
> making them flow,
> like a great, shadowy river,
> with meandering tributaries
> across the lush lawn.

I think of such poems as "freeze frame" poems, a pause in living to note life itself. The literal description of the above view metamorphoses into a poem with the addition of various literary elements and techniques that characterize poetry.

Thus, with the above defining characteristics in mind, compare the poem "Majesty" (above) with this merely literal description of the same view:

> On the lawn, the shadow of an old tree reminds me of
> a wide river with many twisted tributaries.

That sentence, though descriptive, does not exactly beg to be read aloud. Although the memory might be a fond one, it is not *lyrical* (like music flowing in one's mind), and certainly not as moving or *resonant* (like an echo that stays with you) as the same description in "Majesty." In the exercises to follow, your students will transform similar memorable, yet literal descriptions into their own poems, with both traditional poetic forms (featuring specified rhythm and rhyme patterns) and free verse forms, such as the one used in "Majesty."

In brief, the literary elements and techniques that define poetry include:

- **Imagery**: Words that evoke memorable images that stimulate the reader's senses, uniquely expressed perceptions that enlighten readers in some way, and unusually vivid word choices.

- **Rhythm and Form**: Established via line breaks, syllable stresses, repeated words, parallel structures, and punctuation, the rhythm and form of a poem create a marriage of the audible (the sounds of the linked words) and the visible (the shape formed by those words on the page).

- **Performable Eloquence**: Like a song, with or without musical accompaniment, a poem begs to be heard, not simply read.

- **Figurative Expressions**: Evocative expressions like similes and metaphors draw unusual comparisons in order to intrigue, surprise, enchant, and/or entertain readers.

- **Repetitive Sounds**: The poet uses repetitive letter sounds (such as in the technique called *alliteration*, in which initial consonant sounds repeat, as in "towering, twisted, old tree") for auditory resonance; in other words, repeated sounds echo in the reader's ears for a memorable dramatic effect. Rhymes constitute one such example of the use of repetitive sounds; aspiring poets ought to note that not all poems must rhyme.

They will also learn how a topic often dictates the poetic form; for example, a ballad-style poem may suit a solemn message, whereas a light-hearted look at friendship might fall into short lines that rhyme. In some of the exercises in this book, students will write two poetic versions of the same concept to explore how they can alter readers' perceptions of a topic simply by altering the means of presentation, and they will observe how this method of changing one's approach applies to all forms of writing.

Poems of all styles often use *analogies*, or comparisons, to evoke mental pictures figuratively and create memorable images, often from a symbolic perspective. Analogies may be obvious to the reader:

> The sand is like crumbled mountains, dissolved by lapping waves.

Or, they may be subtle:

> ### *Sands of Time*
> Former mountain fortresses,
> eroded by the sea;

the children now rebuild your grains
into tiny castles,
still threatened by the tides of change.

The obvious type of figurative comparison, called a *simile*, shows how one thing is similar to another by using the words *like* or *as*. Comparisons made with similes usually require little or no backtracking from the reader for understanding. In the simile above, one immediately recognizes that sand is compared to crumbled mountains. The more subtle *metaphor* (meta-, the prefix, means "after" or "beyond") leaves perceptive readers with clues that may occur to them after they read the passage, sometimes more than once. Metaphors are neither obvious nor instantly understood, and thus, they transport readers beyond the concrete, to the abstract plane of thought. The sample metaphorical poem, "Sands of Time," presents the sand's evolutionary role in history, implying that each grain forms part of a larger whole, its purpose changing in form, but not necessarily in substance. A metaphor often forces readers to backtrack, or reread, before uttering an "Aha!"

Using Christina Rossetti's short metaphorical poem, "Clouds," as my own poetic inspiration, I wrote this poem specifically as a prompt for my students:

Cumulus Potatoes

Mashed potatoes on blue gravy,
stirred by wind,
the clumps grow wavy,
Stretching, thinning,
slurped by sky,
leaving strands through which birds fly.

I was lucky enough to find in my photograph prompt collection a picture of a sky that matched my poem. My workshop students listened to the poem while looking at the sky photograph and then each chose from my collection of nature photographs a picture to convey in a similarly metaphorical fashion. The results astounded me: A photo of a palm tree's shadow on a smooth beach was portrayed as a black spider spreading across the sand as it baked in the hot sun, and then got washed away by the tide in the sunset (that came from a 7-year-old). Another poem, by a 9-year-old, evolved from a photographic prompt of a murky, green, tropical swamp; the young writer showed with words a green snake slithering between spindly trees.

Some poems use analogies to evoke thoughts about related themes and highlight the connections between seemingly dissimilar concepts or images. Poetry, in this way, can show how much all humans have in common. The following poem, written when I was in high school (years before I had experienced pregnancy) seems to me today no less apt a description for the birthing of a poem now that I have actually had three children.

Pregnant Mind

I was born with child,
grew up giving birth,
my life one endless pregnancy;
and infinite mass of poetic embryos
suspended within a cerebral sac,
feeding on the perceptions and emotions
of experience.
They kick me inside to let them out,
until the first inspiration hits,
and my mind goes into labor;
my breath quickens with my pen,
and I sigh as I push my offspring out,
onto a paper cradle,
to be nurtured
and grown.
Ahhh, it's that time again—
another poem is born.

Having had no experience with birth at the time that poem was written did not affect the emotion conveyed, for I drew upon the feeling of emotional release, the exhausting and exhilarating creation of a poem. Thus, an emotionally similar event can allow both author and reader to experience a kind of virtual reality.

I often tell my students to draw upon their "emotional memory banks" in writing scenes for a reader to experience fully. I asked one student to write about a time when he was flying an airplane and discovered that all of his emergency lights began flashing, and that he had lost control of the plane. "How can I write about that, Mrs. Lipson?" he asked. "I've never flown a plane!" I asked whether he had ever felt out of control, physically, in a situation that threatened his safety. I told him to use that feeling from his emotional memory bank to create the airplane scene. A light bulb seemed to ignite over his head as he replied, "Ah! Can I use the time I lost control of my bike while I was riding down a steep hill?" He could, and he did. He began thinking like a poet, using multisensory imagery to stimulate his readers' senses and connect the DVD playing in his brain with the DVD player in the reader's brain. His airplane disaster piece conveyed the helplessness of someone futilely attempting to regain control of a vehicle. Although neither the prompt nor the assignment involved a poem, the lesson was based on poetic principles. Inform your students that, in the lessons that follow, they may also write prose in response to the provided prompts of poetry, which will give them more insight into the relative powers of various forms of self-expression.

Some poetry offers powerful social commentary by using irony—the figurative use of words to signify the opposite of their literal meaning. *Irony*, when used well, can make the reader smile knowingly at the sarcastic tone, nod in agreement, or perhaps even laugh aloud. I wrote the following poem, a sonnet, in response to a thematically similar one by Robert Frost (1915) called, "Mending Wall."

Neighborly Love

In ancient days, no doors were ever locked,
And silversmiths had not invented keys;
If Man had visitors, they never knocked,
For loving neighbors made him feel at ease.
And then, one day, Man found his home was robbed;
Some thief had emptied all his walls and floors;
When neighbors heard, the silversmiths were mobbed—
The whole town asked for locks to bar their doors.
They left for church each Sunday with their keys,
To listen to the teachings of their Lord,
And "Love thy neighbor" had been one of these—
They'd seen it in their Bibles, locked and stored.
Now when a neighbor visits Man, he knocks,
For what makes loving neighbors but good locks?

In explaining the writing tool of irony to children, I often say, "Irony is seen in the kinds of lines we'd follow with an exclamation of 'Not!' or 'Yeah, right!'" Poetry and its tools need not be presented as old-fashioned writing, or "just stuff we read in school." Poetry is contemporary in any time.

Some poems use plays on words to heighten meaning, such as *puns* (words with two or more definitions, like the punch lines of many jokes), and expressions with *double meanings*. The poem below, about teaching writing techniques to a young student, plays on the writing teacher's constant reminder to "show, don't tell."

Now That's "Showing" Writing!

When my student,
after silently scribbling
a steady stream
of lead-formed,
but not at all leaden,
ideas,
finally looks up from his paper,
eyes glazed as if just waking up,
or experiencing an awakening,
and drops his pencil on the table
with a sigh—
contentment?
relief?

> exhilarating exhaustion?—
> then I know,
> I know I've shown him how,
> because he's SHOWING,
> not telling,
> me.

The feeling that inspired that poem echoes the sigh emitted by the student, a feeling of both contentment and relief, which I have attempted to show here.

Poetry has a power unlike that of prose. Its power lies, ironically, in its limitations. Because poetry is limited to fewer words than prose permits, and to a defined structure, the poet must focus on the power and purpose of each word. As writer Jules Renard once said, "The less you write, the better it must be."

As you complete each of the following lessons with your students, call their attention to word choices. Your focus will be directed to this aspect of writing, both in poetry and prose, in the analytical questions that follow each poem. Remind them that their words should not simply fill paper, but rather, ought to enrich it—along with the eyes and minds that read them.

D.A.D. and M.O.M.: Memorable Guides to Improve All Forms of Writing

D.A.D. and M.O.M. will help any writer improve all forms of writing—but I'm not talking about parents. Rather, I'm talking about two mnemonic devices (memory assisting techniques) that remind writers to include six specific elements for livelier writing. Both the D.A.D. and M.O.M. writing techniques are described below.

D.A.D. Technique

To show, rather than merely tell readers about a scene, writers should include description, action, and dialogue (though not necessarily in that order).

D.A.D. = Description, Action, Dialogue

Description refers not only to adjectives, but also to similes and metaphors, or comparisons that help the reader experience what the author imagined while writing the scene. The descriptions ought to stimulate more than one of the reader's five senses. For example: "The *turquoise* surf *crashed* onto the *marbled* sand, spewing *hissing white foam* that *tickled* and *chilled* my bare toes." The italicized descriptions appeal to the reader's senses of sight, hearing, and touch, allowing the reader to experience, not just read about, the scene. Descriptions should use specific words that show, rather than merely tell about, an image. Words that express an author's opinion—like *ugly* or *beautiful*—describe nothing; what's ugly to one reader may be called beautiful by another. A specific description will allow the reader to form his or her own mental images, images with depth not found in mere opinion words.

Action refers to the use of vivid verbs to show actions that enrich the written conversations and help the reader understand more about the characters in a story. Actions come to life when vivid verbs, such as *strolled*, replace "blah" verbs, such as *went*. Likewise, actions jump off the page when one substitutes active verbs for passive ones; for example, instead of "he was a lot taller than Kim," one could write "he towered over Kim." Relying too heavily on adverbs to enliven "blah" verbs creates stiff, "telling" prose. For instance, rather than tell the reader that a character "looked curiously at his little sister's eyes and asked her kindly whether she had been crying and why," show that he "leaned forward, squinting at his sister's puffy, red eyes, as he smoothed her bangs off of her forehead. He whispered, 'Hey, li'l sis, whatsa matter? Have you been crying?'" Vague verbs can also have multiple meanings, depending on the reader, and writers can eliminate confusion by showing a scene with very specific actions and dialogue.

Dialogue, as shown above, serves as a far more active method of showing what characters say rather than simply telling about what they say. A well-written dialogue enables readers to enter the scene and hear it for themselves. When a writer merely tells about what people say, he or she removes readers from the scene and dulls their interest in the characters' situations. Dialogue ought to reflect character traits and move the story along. Eliminate words that do nothing to advance the story or help the reader understand the characters better. The readers need not hear lines like "I assume that you would rather not have cereal for breakfast, or toast and eggs, or oatmeal, but rather, your usual favorite, cold pizza," when those readers could hear instead: "Let me guess—cold pizza for breakfast again?" Dialogue should sound the way people talk, which means that grammar rules may not always apply to words within quotation marks that represent a written conversation.

All three elements in the D.A.D. technique build upon each other. They don't have to appear in order, nor do they have to appear together in every paragraph. However, truly memorable fiction usually includes description, action, and dialogue on most pages (even if the dialogue is a person talking to him- or herself). Examine favorite stories and novels—the ones that created virtual movies that still play in the reader's mind when recalled—and one will see the important role of D.A.D.

As for nonfiction, vivid writing has as much importance as it does in fiction, and the D.A.D. technique will liven up essays, reports, and articles, too. You may be saying to yourself, "Sure, I understand how one can use description and action in creative nonfiction . . . but dialogue?" Simply remind students to include words spoken by others (i.e., quotations) to illustrate their points. And, when guiding their revisions of nonfiction and checking for the D.A.D. elements, have them look for quotation marks to ensure that they have painted a vivid nonfiction word picture. Using the D.A.D. technique in all forms of writing will immediately improve written works, whether they are fiction, poetry, or nonfiction.

M.O.M. Technique

Now, for the M.O.M. technique, a second, more advanced step to further enrich artistry with words.

M.O.M. = Mood, Order, Matter

Mood refers to the tone of a piece of writing. Word choices affect how a reader perceives the images or imaginary world that a writer has created. How one chooses D.A.D. elements will determine the mood of a work, and writers often have to alter the descriptions, actions, and/or dialogues to fit the mood they hope to convey. For example, to set a mysterious mood, one might describe a garden as "shrouded in mist"; a man's action as "shifting his eyes back and forth as he tiptoed through the garden"; and that man's dialogue lines might read: "Where on earth could he have hidden?" Similarly, those basic elements would change for a scary story. For instance, the garden might feature a description of "a hedge of twisted junipers, contorted like writhing, green monsters." The same scary story might show the man's actions as: "He sweated profusely as he darted between rows of thorny stems and spider-like tendrils," and his dialogue lines might read: "This can't be real—heaven help me, it can't!" One word alone can alter a piece's mood. Consider these two sentences, differing only in verb choices, one showing us a happy scene, and the other showing us a sad or troubled mood.

> Sam skipped around the park.
> Sam trudged around the park.

Students can experiment with other verbs that can change the mood of this sentence, not to mention the image of Sam. Thus, mood, the first element of the M.O.M. technique, both enriches and depends upon D.A.D.

In nonfiction, think of mood as the tone writers set using either formal or informal words. In an essay written to persuade (convince) the reader of the author's personal opinion about something, it is sometimes appropriate to "talk" directly to the reader and use contractions (e.g., "it's" instead of "it is"), rather than very formal wording. In a report of information, in which one presents only facts and no opinion, the mood must remain objective, like a factual newspaper article.

Order refers to the order in which a work supplies information to the reader. If a story grows from a specific setting—such as a creepy old mansion—and the author wishes to introduce the characters slowly, as they enter the mansion, building the reader's suspense, then the opening must rely heavily on the element of description. The author might decide to change that order if he or she prefers to speed up the plot and engage the reader in action from the first line, rather than risk boring him or her with a lengthy description of the mansion. The order in which a story presents the D.A.D. elements will determine how that work affects readers—whether the author offers subtle hints about the plot in advance, perhaps even revealing the end scene at the start, and then keeping the reader guessing all along about how that ending will occur; or the story might supply intriguing tidbits of description or deceptive dialogue to keep the reader wondering about the character's true personality. Call students' attention to the order of the story elements when you read works as a class. Discuss what would have happened if an author had ordered the elements differently. Have students experiment with changing the order of elements as they revise stories, poems, nonfiction narrative pieces, and essays. In nonfiction, the order of the main points, and the summation of those points in the end, determines whether a reader comes away from a piece feeling well-informed or confused, convinced or bored.

Matter, the final element of M.O.M., means two things: First, I mean matter as the substance or stuff we write about, and, second, I mean matter as having a definite purpose. Thus, the matter consists of all those details that absolutely must appear on the page in order for the reader to understand the meaning of the entire piece. If writers add unnecessary artistic details that don't matter to the reader's understanding, then they decrease the power of the matter and confuse the reader. As Shakespeare wrote in *Hamlet*, "More matter, less art." Deciding which matter matters is what we do in the final editing stage of the writing process, in which we delete superfluous words that slow down, or distract from, the work's purpose. The matter, order, and mood all influence each other in writing, and we must show students the importance of each element in the writing process.

Final Thoughts

Remind students (and yourself) to heed D.A.D. and M.O.M. when writing, and they will certainly show progress—I guarantee it. (They will also learn to appreciate, as readers, the effective use of these techniques by their favorite authors.) I advise my students before they revise to jot the letters *D*, *A*, and *D* vertically in the margin of their first draft, as a checklist. As they reread each page, they check off the elements of description, action, and dialogue, and then add and/or subtract lines to create a balance between those elements.

In using the checklist, they may find that their fiction is too heavy on dialogue and light on description, or their nonfiction is too heavy on description and lacking illustrative quotations (dialogue). In any case, if you use D.A.D. this way to guide their completion of each second draft, you will then have prepared manuscripts ready for M.O.M.'s editorial guidance. Thus, referring to D.A.D. and M.O.M. in writing instruction will create writings worth remembering.

A student handout about D.A.D. and M.O.M., to be saved for continual reference, appears on page 31.

The Poetry Prompts

Each exercise is skills-based, and students will experiment with many different styles and genres of writing. Poems have been grouped, as much as possible, by themes (e.g., nature, social commentary, friendship, love).

Every lesson offers a poem (or two comparable poems), followed by discussion questions and/or comments to guide or deepen the reader's understanding of the piece. Read all of the exercises and extension exercises before choosing to work with each prompt. In some cases, you may suggest or assign extensions without having students do the preceding exercises. However, some of the exercises build upon each other and require that students complete them in consecutive order.

All of the lessons enrich interrelated skills, allowing for a spiral approach to the skill-building process. By touching upon a concept, and then coming full circle to enrich that concept on another level via extension exercises, students experience process-oriented learning that focuses on continued growth, rather than on individual products. Sure, a "do-A-and-B-to-produce-C" approach may create a portfolio of writings, but it will not create competence in writing. Competence comes from approaching each writing assignment as a learning opportunity, and not simply as a job to complete.

You may want to have your students purchase binders in which to keep all—every draft of every piece—of the writing they will do via *Writing Success Through Poetry*. They will need each draft to get the most out of this program, which requires in the final extension exercise for the poem "Revision" an analysis of their individual progress by comparing their first drafts to their final drafts. Even if students do not complete all of the exercises in this book, they should complete the final extension exercise as a means of evaluating individual progress.

Every piece of writing can be recycled in the following educational ways: (a) for an editing lesson, (b) for expansion of a piece with potential for further development (e.g., a brief dialogue might evolve into a short story, or a descriptive paragraph might turn into a poem), (c) for a complete revision to try a new style on an old idea (a change in point of view can sometimes give new life to an old story), and (d) for a source of practical spelling words that have shown up as misspellings in the students' own works. Students can learn as much, or more, from studying their *own* writings with a critical eye than from studying other authors' works.

Student Examples Written in Response to the Poetry Prompts

The students' works that follow may serve as additional prompts or merely as models for your own students' writing exercises. The poetry prompt that inspired each new poem is listed above each title.

Written in response to "Beach Party" (see p. 38).

Sticks, Stones, Broken Bones
By Elliot Shin, age 14

Cutting, splashing,
Showering, streaming,
Raining, hailing,
Drenching, and pelting.
The rain and hail gather,
Weeping down from pregnant skies.
Eroding soil, molding mud.
Pieces of gravel are misplaced,
by falling drops of water,
But one grows only bolder.
The soil seeps away from its edges,
Crawling away for its task had failed.
Naught moves this boulder,
Naught wets this boulder,
Naught soaks into this boulder.
Try as they might, they cannot wet it,
They cannot affect it with their touch,
Cannot hurt it, cannot scar it,
Not even with words.

I can't recall whether the "sticks and stones may break my bones . . ." chant first inspired this response to "Beach Party," or whether the impetus was the idea of a rock's ability to deflect assaults. In any case, Elliot's metaphorical idea conveys his own "hardening" to the harsh words that other teenagers can sometimes inflict upon their peers. The angry rain of verbal assaults comes at the reader via vivid verbs: cutting, showering, hailing, and pelting. I admire his use of erosion as a metaphor for the breaking down of the human spirit, and the image of "molding mud" to show how people sometimes recast themselves in response to how others treat them. The line "But one only grows bolder" refers, of course, to the "one" who narrates, who toughens himself, and it has additional impact due to the pun with the homophone "boulder." Elliot raised his eyebrows and chuckled when I pointed out the pun, which he did not plan, at least consciously. When asked why he chose the archaic "naught" as a repetitive word, Elliot shrugged and told me that it simply fit the tone somehow. The final line, regarding the powerlessness of forceful words against him, relates subtly and skillfully to the childhood chant from the title. Like "Beach Party," Elliot's "Sticks, Stones, Broken Bones" conveys metaphorically the universal outcast feeling known by most adolescents at some time during the high school years.

Written in response to "Beach Party" (see p. 38).

The Teased Deer

By Jenny Tsai, age 11

I am a deer
Who runs from any predator that I see.
You build traps of embarrassment in the forest
And try to attract me into them.
I try to stay away from you
And sniff around for dangerous traps.
I try to blend in with my surroundings,
Yet you still manage to find me.
Why me? Why not another deer?
You follow me around like an evil spirit.
You carry intimidating weapons with you
And I almost never earn a time
When I can catch a breath
Away from you.

The same prompt, "Beach Party," given to a younger student here, evokes a piece that reflects the anxiety felt by a victim of a bully—in this case, a "predator." The deer serves as the perfect animal for this personification, with its gentleness and its nervousness, and its avoidance of "traps of embarrassment" set for the timid creature. The idea of her camouflaging herself within her surroundings fits very well in this context, for both a deer and a shy girl will strive for invisibility in the presence of predators. Jenny speaks to most kids her age in this profoundly touching poem.

Written in response to "Blinded by Sight" (see p. 41).

A Colorless Sunset

by Ian Lipson, age 11

Warm sand under my feet,
A comforting feeling throughout my body.
I hear "oohs" and "awes"

As surrounding families stare
And marvel at the scene.
"Look, Ma, it's like a collage of reds, pinks, orange, and yellow
floating in the sky,"
I hear from a child next to me,
Enjoying the sunset with his family.
The crisp, but smooth sound of seagulls circling the colors
That others can see, but I can't . . .
To me this scene is colorless
But beautiful,
A beautiful blankness.
But, I share the same beauty
In a different way,
With different senses.
It brought back amazing memories
Of how I used to sit with my family
On the beach,
Marveling and enjoying all the colors
Of such a wondrous sight.

Ian focused on the imagery available to a blind narrator, in this vivid description of a sunset at the beach. His use of alliteration in the memorable description of the "crisp, but smooth sound of seagulls circling" (notice all the *s* sounds) almost carries through the poem a background of soft "sssss-ing," like lapping waves. I also appreciated his accidental pun in the words "'oohs' and 'awes'"—instead of "aahs"—implying the emotion of the sunset viewers. His additional alliterative expression "beautiful blankness" might even have worked as a title, although his title is intriguing.

It took a couple of drafts to eliminate details that would have required the narrator to have sight. He was asked questions such as, "But, you wrote that the child is watching the sunset with his family; how do you, a blind person, know that they're watching?" That prompted Ian to add the child's spoken words to his poem, which show, rather than tell, that the child observes the sunset. Ian enjoyed the challenge of description without the sense—vision—that most written descriptions rely upon most. His enjoyment now passes to his readers with this sensually rich, touching poem.

Written in response to "Knock, Knock . . . Who's There?" (see p. 44).

Rolling With Laughter
By Elle Lipson, age 12

A giggle, a cackle, a hearty guffaw,
A timid squawk, or a noisy caw;

A laugh can tell what someone feels,
A laugh can be joyous, embarrassed, concealed . . .

My sister's laugh is a bubbly giggle;
When she laughs, she snorts and wiggles;
Her laugh burbles like the babbling creek
On my nature alarm clock, long and deep.

My brother erupts a snorting laugh,
When he guffaws, he rolls and gasps.
He laughs uncontrollably, leaning on me,
A pleasant hyena, cackling with glee.

My mom's laugh is an all-out squawk;
She tumbles around, unable to talk.
Her laugh pours out until she cries,
Merry tears flow from her eyes.

My dad's laugh is a treasure so rare—
A chuckle emanating from his every hair!
It grows to a rumble, soaked with mirth,
And grows to an even greater girth!

Laughing, guffawing, giggling,
Chuckling, tearing, wiggling;
Soon, my whole family rolls around,
Rolling with laughter on the ground!

The prompt emphasizes sound power—how various sounds affect us in different ways. When Elle read her first draft of this poem aloud, a moment of silence followed her last line before everyone started clapping loudly and oohing and aahing. The audience saw how the absence of sound (the awed silence, in this case) can contain as much power as a sound (the enthusiastic applause) releases into the air. The listeners' responses prompted Elle to submit the poem to *Creative Kids*, and the magazine started her career as an official published author.

Written in response to "Knock, Knock . . . Who's There?" (see p. 44).

Who's on the Phone?

By Ishan Sengupta, age 13

"Hello?"
"Wasssssssssssssssssup!?!"
Who's on the phone?
Someone who knows me well;
A friend who just can't wait to tell me something;
Or perhaps an ambitious salesperson who wants
to get on my good side before I hang up?

"Hello?"
"............................"
Who was on the phone?
Someone who realized that this was the wrong
number;
A friend who found that he couldn't talk right
now;
Or maybe a seller who figures I am not the kind of
person to buy perfume?

"Hello?"
"ConGraTuLaTions! You have Won . . ."
Who or what is on the phone?
Someone trying to ploy me into a deal by saying I
won something;
A friend who wants to tell me that I won the draw-
ing at school;
Or possibly a machine that was programmed to
sell me items for free, although it ends with "Re-
StricTions will Apply."

"Hello?"
"Hi, I live across . . . (giggle) . . . the street and
well, your daughter . . . (snort) . . . kicked my dog
. . ."
Who's on the phone?
Someone who has free time and wants to have a
little fun;
A friend who likes to prank before he talks;
Or even a merchant who wants to sell me Caller
ID so I know who to hang up on?

"Hello?"
"Hey, Ishan!"
Who's on the phone?
Someone who knows me and wanted to get in
touch;
A friend who recognizes my voice;
But I know it is not a salesperson, and for this I
am happy.

"Hello?"
"??????????"
Listen to the reply.
You may find out who it is before you ask,
"Who's on the phone?"

Ishan is a master of imitation, for he emulated the prompt poem's structure and style. However, he still made this his own poem

with his vivid, unique images that stay with his readers after they finish reading his work. Notice how the images he chose reflect him, as the narrator. We learn a lot about authors, as well as characters, via the imagery they choose to convey.

Written in response to "Nana's Ring" (see p. 50).

Bedtime With Mommy and Bun Bun

by Sara Huang, age 11

Let's cuddle, Bun Bun,
And think of the times she cuddled us.
Let's wait in bed for her to tuck us in,
Kisses on my cheek and then on yours.
I'll hold you tight, in the dark,
Just like she did for me.
You hold a warmth in my heart,
Reminding me of her.
So let's wait,
and she'll come to kiss us good night.
My eyes shut, yours forever open.

The new, green walls turn white.
Now I'm back to the time
when she stayed with us through the night.
Your fake fur, against my skin.
My skin, against hers.
Your bell, silenced as we lie still.
I gripped you, feeling the stuffing inside,
Down to the middle,
grasping the bell in your stomach.
Your ducky pajamas,
the same as always,
matching the middles of your long,
bunny ears, perfectly stitched,
just like the ears of the two bunnies that you have
for feet.

Footsteps awaken me from this dream,
But, I'm still waiting for her to come in and kiss
me good night.
Don't worry, Bun Bun, for soon I will sleep,
And she will come in at last.
Maybe then, you will shut your eyes,
And dream of her arms around us both.

Sara's cozy scene comes to life via multisensory imagery: We see, hear, and feel the bedtime moment with her. Her personification of Bun Bun makes the stuffed animal come alive as a symbol of her fleeting childhood. She creates a subtle, skillful transition from present to past, via her description: "The new, green walls turn white / Now I'm back to the time . . ." Like a filmmaker zooming in on the walls to show the audience that time has passed, Sara focused on a single element in her scene as a tool for showing a time shift. Bun-Bun's intangible value, like Nana's ring in the original prompt, obviously gives the narrator a feeling of fulfillment and peace.

Written in response to "Thirsty Plant and Cloudy Sky" (Further Extension A; see pp. 52–53).

Stubborn Man

By Lainey Lipson, age 11

"Will you please help me with this?" Sharon asked, while struggling to pick up one of the boxes.

"Now?" he replied.

"Come on, Jim, watching TV isn't nearly as important!"

"But, my favorite show is on!" exclaimed Jimmy, frustrated.

Sharon's pale, skinny arms, lined with out-popping veins, strained to hold the heavy box. "It's not like this is the last time they're ever going to play this episode! Jeez!" Sharon put down the box and picked up the clicker, and turned off the TV.

Jim glared at her with his big, blue eyes. "Fine . . . whatever."

He put the smaller box of the two into Sharon's cradled arms, and left the bigger one for himself. They slowly trudged outside with their aching arms wrapped around the boxes. Jim dropped his box on the ground and let out a big sigh of relief.

"Ha! And you thought I was the weak one!" Sharon exclaimed joyfully. "Let's take out the pieces."

He reached into his pocket and pulled out his pocketknife and sliced through the tape on the boxes. They both sat on the ground, put their feet on the box, and yanked out the bubble-wrapped pieces of waterslide.

"Wow! This is huge!" Sharon shrieked. They unwrapped the slide and began to set it up. "Think how happy Jen is gonna be!" she exclaimed.

Lainey decorated the given skeletal dialogue lines (i.e., "Will you help me with this?" she asked, and "Now?" he replied) with ample description and action, forming a lively scene between a wife and a husband. I especially enjoyed the visually rich detail of the couple sitting on the ground, with their feet on their boxes, yanking out bubble-wrapped pieces of a waterslide. The dialogue creates a mood of friendly rivalry in the end ("Ha! And you thought I was the weak one!") that has far more interest for a reader than a simple discussion about him helping her unload the boxes. Active verbs like *trudged* and *glared* and *yanked* add life to this scene and reflect the author's care in selecting words.

Written in response to "Life as a Tree" (see p. 55).

Life as the Sun

By Carrie Chen, age 10

Our lives would be so much better,
If we all lived like the sun.
Always there when everyone needs us,
Just like a reliable friend.
It gives you warmth,
A good feeling inside,
A feeling so good that no one can hide.
And as it flashes its brilliant rays at you,
It makes you feel happy and glowing within,
And puts a smile on your face.
Shining so bright,
It makes you feel tall and strong,
Like when you've accomplished something you've
never before accomplished.
Reliable, warm, and bright,
What could ever be a better model than the sun?

Carrie's poem uses personification to portray her ideal friend: someone warm, reliable, brilliant, inspiring, and supportive. She definitely "got" this prompt and showed obvious pride in her ability to see the sun as a symbolic role model. This poem, like the sun, made her feel "tall and strong / like when you've accomplished something you've never before accomplished." Figurative thinking and its translation into original metaphors adds magic to writing, especially for students who once read in primarily literal terms.

Written in response to "A Fly That Tried" (see p. 61).

Evil

By Uyen Bui, age 11

Serena spotted six silvery spiders.
"Eek! Eek!" she screeched.
SIX SMALL SILVERY SPIDERS!
"Kill! Kill!" she barked.
Serena swiped seven sticks.
Bam! Bam! She tried to kill the spiders.
"Hea! Hea! Ha! Ha!" Serena laughed.
"Gotcha! Gotcha!"
"Don-Don Don Don!" she sang "Beethoven's Fifth."
Six silvery spiders sprinted to safety.
"Found you all!"
Smush!
"Oh, I'm so sorry!"
"NOT!"

Uyen's first attempt to show a person's character by the way she reacts to spiders made her classmates giggle, especially with her dramatic reading, enhanced by a devilish grin. The listeners appreciated her use of alliteration, which, with its repetitive *s* sounds, echoed like a sinister hiss, perfectly setting the mood of this "evil" poem. She was then challenged to paint a character portrait of a spider-lover, to contrast with the first poem. She did, as follows:

Live: The Mirror Image of Evil

By Uyen Bui

Serena spotted six silvery spiders.
"Ahh! Ahh! Spiders!" she panicked.
"Such small spiders!" Serena thought.
"Oh! Oh! Come here, come here!" she urged.
"I'll keep you safe!" Serena ensured.
Six silvery spiders sensed safety from Serena.
They sprinted onto her hand.
"You'll be all right!" Serena sang.
Creak! Creak! Creak! She opened the door.
Her fingers flicked them onto the foliage.
Six silvery spiders sprinted to safety.

Uyen's spider-lover "sang" and "ensured," rather than "screeched" or "barked," as in the first poem. Her word choices reflect very different moods, and somehow the alliteration sounds soothing now, instead of sinister.

More Ideas for Prompts

- *Idea-driven prompts*: quotations, overheard conversations, and comments left unsaid.

    Have students open any quotation book, and find a passage to *show*, either as fiction or a poem, or as a concept to illustrate in an essay. Students may enjoy jotting down snippets of conversations overheard in a restaurant, while standing in a line somewhere, at a store, and so forth—words overheard by accident (eavesdropping is not recommended!)—and using such lines as the basis for an imaginary conversation, a dialogue in a new story. Recall an intriguing conversation, in which someone could have replied differently, and give that person a new reply by writing a similar dialogue and making it end differently than it did.

    Example of a quotation prompt: Some high school students were asked to respond in writing to this thought-provoking quotation that was heard on the radio: "Race is a cultural construct." After discussing their interpretations of the quotation's meaning, they brainstormed specific examples to illustrate the themes that had been discussed. Finally, they all wrote four-paragraph essays, opening with that quotation.

• *Plot-driven prompts*: objects, news stories, recycled story openers, and Conflict Cards.

Collect a bagful of miscellaneous objects (no more than 10), and allow students to turn them into a story by randomly drawing three from the bag and imagining them as props in a story. First, determine who might possess or find these objects, and why that character would use, treasure, or perhaps, lose one or more of the items. Write about how the items influence some action or reaction from the character. It's amazing how a story can form from adding a character to own these items.

With news stories, borrow a conflict from real life and modify the details, add new characters, and magically cook up a new tale, based on reality. Remember to change the details and the names of real people to make it fictional.

Recycling story openers can lead to a story: Take an interesting opening from a published story or novel, and continue the story in an entirely new way. After writing the tale, replace the recycled opening with the new opening (for we never want to plagiarize, no matter how few lines we borrow. Remind students that plagiarism is stealing when using someone's hard-earned words without permission; it is an actual crime.).

Another fun plot-driven prompt: Give all of your students an index card and have them label one side *Conflict Card*, and on the other side, have them write a short phrase (such as "stuck having lunch with a rude person," "discovering a secret about one's teacher," or "a bike accident") as a plot-driven prompts. Collect and shuffle the cards, then pass out one card to each student and ask him or her to write a short story driven by the conflict on the assigned card.

• *Character-driven prompts*: telephone directory used for character names and settings (the Yellow Pages ads), magazine model photographs, yearbook pictures, old family photographs, and names drawn from other books and newspapers. Art featuring people and suggesting emotions, relationships, or unstated words can also inspire students.

Have students open a telephone directory, close their eyes, and point— this is a great way to find a new character name. Try the advertisement pages to find a setting for the story; for example, an auto repair shop ad can turn into a story about a person who needs auto repairs after a serious accident.

For photograph prompts, select pictures that reveal emotions in the faces of people. A simple smiling pose won't evoke the same level of story ideas as one in which the person shows some emotion in the facial expression.

Some leading opening lines for developing a character-driven story include:

- He's at it again.
- Politeness was definitely not her middle name.
- She waved goodbye without a single tear.
- She had, unfortunately, learned not to say "See you later!" after kissing her family members good-bye each morning.
- He controlled her; she controlled me; and I had no control over anything.
- Nothing could have hurt me more—nothing.
- Waiting, he was always waiting.
- The trouble started with the party.
- "So what?" he replied casually to the startling news.

- *Revision-driven prompts*: Have students take out their own past works, see them in a new light, and rewrite. At least a third of the poems in this book sound a lot different from their original versions, written years ago. Some of my oldest poems inspired some of the brand-new ones in this collection, too. Students can create new treasures based on raw jewels created months ago.

A Note to Students

The purpose of writing is communication. If you have something to say, make sure you do so in as few words as possible so as not to waste paper. Write what needs expressing; write with a purpose; write to communicate ideas to a reader, not just to yourself; and write because you can add your own thoughts to the greater body of knowledge. Write to say something, not just to fill pages and get a grade.

The comments jotted in margins by a thoughtful teacher have far more bearing on your development as a writer than any grade will ever have. Save every comment-filled work you receive, so that you can refer back to that work later. Even if some comments seem off-base to you, consider that they express the way your words were perceived by your reader—whether or not you intended it to be that way. Consider that a misperception by the reader indicates that you might not have expressed yourself as clearly as you could have; thus, rewriting might be necessary. Now, not all comments from a reader will seem worthy of your consideration for a rewrite, but you will learn to assess their worthiness with time, experience, and confidence in your own standards for your personal best.

If you already have the confidence to know what truly amounts to your best work, then the grade should have little meaning to your development as a writer. I often tell the following story to audiences of students: In high school, I had a teacher who always provided feedback in the margins of my work, and who always gave me A's on my papers. The one time I threw together a lousy essay (I waited until the morning the paper was due!), I received, nevertheless, an A from the teacher and no written comments. I suspected that he had been as lazy as I had, and that he hadn't actually read my paper, but had merely assigned an A to it based on past experience with my work. I asked him whether he had read my paper, and he replied, blushing, "I gave you an A, didn't I?" I said that I couldn't imagine why I'd received an A on what was definitely not my usual standard of work. With his graying eyebrows raised, he countered, "Are you actually asking that I lower your grade?" I said that I was asking him to read my paper again and make his own decision, because in my opinion, this A made all my other truly deserved A's seem less impressive to me. He asked me what grade I'd have given my current essay, and then I was the one to blush; I told him "C." My teacher ended up giving me a "B-, because you were honest," and he remarked, "That's the first time any student has actually complained about getting an A." You may not believe this, but I did feel better, more justified, with that B-, because I knew that my other A's now counted. My point, however, is not about grades; it's about standards, and knowing what really defines your current best. I say *current* because your best should always be changing as you grow as a writer and improve your techniques. So, *best* refers to the most accomplished work at that particular time in your life. Always do your best. It's yours, not someone else's standard, that counts.

—S. L. Lipson

Writing With D.A.D. and M.O.M.: Student Guide to the Three-Step Writing Process

Step 1: Write the first draft with D.A.D. (for words that show, rather than merely tell). Use each of the following D.A.D. elements, in any order:

D.A.D. = Description, **A**ction, and **D**ialogue

- **Description**: Colorful adjectives and illustrative phrases, such as similes and metaphors; words that affect two or more of the reader's five senses.
- **Action**: Vivid verbs that show action, not tell about it; active verbs that bring descriptions to life. (Avoid using passive verbs, such as: *am, is, are, was, were, be, being, been, go, goes, went, do, does, did.*)
- **Dialogue**: Written conversations between characters, punctuated by quotation marks; words spoken silently by a character to him- or herself, printed in italics or underlined; and quoted words (in non-fiction writing) punctuated by quotation marks and followed with a reference to the printed source of the words).

Step 2: Revise the first draft with M.O.M. Check your first draft for all three D.A.D. elements and revise by adding what you forgot. Now look at your work in terms of the M.O.M. technique.

M.O.M. = Mood, **O**rder, and **M**atter

- **Mood**: Words that convey an appropriate mood, point-of-view, or tone for the specific subject, theme, and style of the writing; for example, emotion-charged words for a suspenseful story, or formal-sounding words for an academic essay.
- **Order**: Material presented in an order suited to the subject, theme, and style; for example, an essay should present the thesis at the end of the introductory paragraph, and a mystery story might present details out of order to keep readers guessing.
- **Matter**: Every word must have a purpose, and if unnecessary, must be deleted. Words must move a story along, or build an essay's main argument.

Checking for the elements of D.A.D. and M.O.M. is the same as editing for substance. After your revisions, you will have a second draft, ready for the final stage of the writing process—proofreading for misspellings and errors in punctuation and grammar.

Copyright ©2006 *Writing Success Through Poetry*, Susan L. Lipson. This page may be photocopied or reproduced with permission for student use.

Poetry Prompt 1

Majesty

Towering, twisted, old tree,
The sun casts new life upon
Your dry, gray limbs,
Making them flow,
Like a great, shadowy river,
With meandering tributaries
Across the lush lawn.

Copyright ©2006 *Writing Success Through Poetry*, Susan L. Lipson. This page may be photocopied or reproduced with permission for student use.

Poetry Prompt 1, continued

For Discussion:

1. What, in this poem, possesses the quality of *majesty*?
2. What other title would you give this poem?
3. Identify one simile, two examples of alliteration, and one example of personification.
4. What is the river? (Hint: Look at its adjectives, and know that the *river* does not refer to part of the tree itself.)
5. Note the adjective *dry*, which describes the tree's limbs. Why do you think the author purposely chose *dry* instead of another word, like *old*?
6. How might the mood, or tone, of this poem have changed if it had been written with rhyme and a defined rhythm?

Exercise: Using either a freeze frame image from your own mind, or a landscape picture or photograph as a prompt, write your own simile-based poem that depicts something in nature as looking like something else (either in nature, or not). You may use a free-verse style or write a rhyming poem—your choice.

Extension Exercise: Write a prose version (one paragraph will do) that describes the same scene you painted in your poem from the exercise above; aim to stimulate in your readers a multisensory response with vivid imagery. Include a simile or two.

Further Extension A: Take either of the written scenes you have "painted" in the poem or the paragraph, and add or substitute a simile or metaphor that simultaneously reveals something about you, the poem's narrator, or some other character in the piece. For example, to "Majesty" the author could add: "The sun casts new life upon/ Your dry, gray limbs,/ Which creak like my own,/ In the teasing breeze. . . ." The reader thus sees the narrator as old and gray, like the tree. When you make a simile do double duty, you practice the economy of words—packing maximum power into a minimum number of words.

Further Extension B: Write two to three paragraphs, supported by specific examples to answer this question: After writing two versions of the same imagery-packed scene, can you now explain how poetry and prose offer different advantages in conveying "word pictures" to the reader?

Copyright ©2006 *Writing Success Through Poetry*, Susan L. Lipson. This page may be photocopied or reproduced with permission for student use.

Poetry Prompt 2

Regal Bonfire Dancers

Tall, spindly, wild-haired silhouettes
Of kings, queens, and fans
Bend and sway
Over sand and surf,
Before the horizon's bonfire,
Moved by both the music of the surf
And the briny, now cool breeze
That feeds the flaming clouds;
They dance in celebration
Of the exquisite struggle
Between Day and Night.

The dancers seem to slow,
As invisible hands
Lower a cool blanket of indigo
Over the fire,
Subduing the embers,
By tucking them into watery darkness,
As the dance scene fades to black.

Copyright ©2006 *Writing Success Through Poetry*, Susan L. Lipson. This page may be photocopied or reproduced with permission for student use.

Poetry Prompt 2, continued

For Discussion:

1. Compare and contrast this poem to "Majesty" (see Poetry Prompt 1), noting how they are similar and how they are different.
2. This freeze frame poem uses *metaphors*. What scene do you "see"?
3. What are the regal bonfire dancers and their fans? Why does this poem describe them as "tall" and "spindly" with "wild hair"? What does the poem mean by "hair"?
4. Explain the use of *personification*.
5. When a scene fades to black in a movie, the sudden darkness marks the end of a dramatic sequence. What makes that line apt for this poem's ending?

Exercise: Write your own beach scene, set in the morning, afternoon, or late at night, to show through carefully chosen details a different view of the beach than this evening sunset view. You may use poetry or prose. Show, don't tell, how the scene looks, smells, sounds, and/or feels to you as an observer. Keep in mind sounds like crickets (mainly heard at night), sights like long shadows versus short shadows (showing the sun's position, and thus the time of day), smells like hot dogs cooking on a barbecue, and feelings like hot sand burning the soles of your feet. Your beach may be populated or uninhabited; your shoreline green, sandy, or rocky; your water full of crashing waves or gentle ripples—it's up to you.

Extension: Turn this literal sentence into a multisensory word picture or poem:
The autumn leaves covering the forest floor make me feel, along with the trees, that winter is coming.

Further Extension A: Write your own literal scene in one or two sentences, as in the extension exercise above, and have a partner do the same. Trade sentences, and create vivid word pictures for each other.

Further Extension B: Draw or paint a picture to illustrate one of your own poetic scenes.

Copyright ©2006 *Writing Success Through Poetry*, Susan L. Lipson. This page may be photocopied or reproduced with permission for student use.

Poetry Prompt 3

Floating Sofa

Like studded, wet leather,
Trimmed in froth,
Glistening in the late summer sunset;
Like a floating sofa rising
above lapping waves,
now black gold.
Rocky studs jut out randomly,
forming ridges for sand crabs
who dare to walk on top of
Mother Earth's furniture
and get grounded—
SO-O grounded!
Reality splashes upon my feet,
turning the leather to sand
and reminding me that
I ought to get home before dark.

Copyright ©2006 *Writing Success Through Poetry*, Susan L. Lipson. This page may be photocopied or reproduced with permission for student use.

Poetry Prompt 3, continued

For Discussion:

1. Can you see the scene that inspired this metaphorical freeze frame poem? What do you see?
2. How old is the narrator of this poem? How do you know?
3. What do you know about the narrator from the word choices?

Exercise: This poem shows how figurative language (such as metaphors and similes) can do double duty by showing something about the character or narrator who uses them, in addition to showing a scene. Create character-revealing similes for the images listed below. Example: falling leaves—"Leaves sprayed the ground in the whirling breeze, like the confetti we tossed at graduation just 6 short months ago." Try to write double-duty similes for at least three of these images:

1. a rainstorm,
2. a spot of purple in a field of browning weeds,
3. a car accident,
4. a rap concert,
5. sore feet, and
6. the smell of roses.

Extension: Expand on the last image above—the smell of roses. Write two very different scenes, beginning with "Janine smelled the roses," to show two very different memories for Janine that have an association with the smell of roses. For instance, perhaps roses remind Janine of her grandmother's funeral, or of a bouquet she received for some achievement. Make sure to use the D.A.D. (Description, Action, Dialogue) technique for each word picture. Your scene needs no more than two paragraphs.

Further Extension A: How a character reacts to a situation shows as much as the situation itself. Reactions also set the tone of a piece and define its genre. Review Janine's reactions in your two scenes from the above extension exercise. Label and title each scene according to its genre. Circle the specific words that set and build the tone.

Further Extension B: Adding point of view to any piece of writing adds depth and enables the reader to "know" the characters. Point of view can be added by using a narrator, or by showing characters through their unique perceptions or actual inner thoughts. Experiment with point of view via two different descriptions of a rock concert (remember to let your reader "hear" the music, too): the point of view of an older person and the point of view of a teenager.

Read these descriptions aloud to your class or a partner, and have them guess which description came from which character. Analyze effectiveness of word choices, and replace vague words with vivid ones.

Copyright ©2006 *Writing Success Through Poetry*, Susan L. Lipson. This page may be photocopied or reproduced with permission for student use.

Poetry Prompt 4

Beach Party

They wade in shallow waters,
laughing and smiling when it's appropriate;
discussing the water temperature
and the height of the waves.
No one seems to notice me,
as I recede into the depths beyond them,
and dive beneath the surface
to see the splendor that awaits.

Sometimes I wish I could always stay,
far below the waders;
maybe then I could finally find
some ancestor of sunken Atlantis,
or at least another diver
to make waves with me.

Copyright ©2006 *Writing Success Through Poetry*, Susan L. Lipson. This page may be photocopied or reproduced with permission for student use.

Poetry Prompt 4, continued

For Discussion:

1. What kind of party does this poem describe? Does it necessarily take place at a beach?
2. Do you see another meaning behind the words? Do you see the metaphor that applies to all parties?
3. Who comprise the waders?
4. Define a diver. Why can't the narrator find other divers?
5. Do you dive or wade at parties? If so, how do you feel?
6. Notice the words *shallow* and *depths*. Consider their double meanings.
7. What splendor awaits the diver in this poem (metaphorically, that is)?
8. Why does the poem refer to Atlantis, other than that it's a sunken civilization? What type of civilization was Atlantis? (Look it up if you don't know.)
   Explain the pun in the last line: "make waves."

Exercise: Write your own poem or short prose description of a party or other social scene from your point of view. You might convey your feelings symbolically, as in the above poem, using a setting to emphasize a thought, such as "shallow waters" to stress the lack of depth of a conversation. You could even write about animals, plants, or objects as symbols for people. Ask yourself whether your work's point of view comes through strongly; if not, enhance it so readers can know how you feel in your heart about the social matter you describe.

Extension: Rewrite the piece you just wrote as a dialogue to show the attitude of either the narrator or a character in the social scene. Convey one character's feeling of isolation within a crowd. Use what you know about feeling different from the crowd. Remember to include description, action, and dialogue in your work.

Further Extension A: Change the actions used to color the dialogue you wrote in the extension exercise to make the words come across differently. For example, look at the difference in the lines below when the action is changed:

> "Oh, yeah, I'm so cool," she bragged, whipping her long,
> silky ponytail over her shoulder.
> "Oh, yeah, I'm so cool," she muttered, rolling her eyes and
> sighing.

Which scene do you prefer? Does this give new meaning to the old saying, "Actions speak louder than words"?

Further Extension B: In one of his songs, Eminem (another kind of poet) has used an apt simile to describe his angry attitude. He has

Copyright ©2006 *Writing Success Through Poetry*, Susan L. Lipson. This page may be photocopied or reproduced with permission for student use.

Poetry Prompt 4, continued

called himself a "pit bull off his leash." Find a simile or metaphor that aptly describes you or someone you know, conveying a specific mood or attitude in the process. For instance, someone might describe a sensitive person as a "roly-poly bug, quickly curling up into himself when he bumps into an obstacle, gently rocking himself to regain his balance, and then unrolling and rolling along, moments later, as though he had never faltered." Try to create similar similes or metaphors for other people you know. Don't hesitate to turn one into a poem if it grows on you.

Copyright ©2006 *Writing Success Through Poetry*, Susan L. Lipson. This page may be photocopied or reproduced with permission for student use.

Poetry Prompt 5

Blinded by Sight

Some say that darkness is the blind man's doom,
But how can one see darkness and not light?
For if there is no sun, there is no moon;
And if there is no day, there is no night.
The blind possess a sense that I do not,
That special sense that aids their inner sight;
In fact, compared to most, they see a lot;
Their visions don't depend on outside light.
The optic nerve is part of Judgment's eye;
Reflected light produces prejudice;
Who's Black or White—the blind cannot decide,
Or who's called "Sir," or "Kid," "Hey You!" or "Miss."
Suppose that eyes were only in one's mind;
Though we'd be sightless, we would not be blind.

Copyright ©2006 *Writing Success Through Poetry*, Susan L. Lipson. This page may be photocopied or reproduced with permission for student use.

Poetry Prompt 5, continued

For Discussion:

1. Puns and plays on words can often make important points and evoke powerful thoughts when used in ironic contexts. *Sonnets*, like this one, often feature such plays on words within their very strictly defined formats (especially in the last two lines, the couplet).
2. What does the second line mean? (Hint: If you've never seen the sky, can you miss it? And, if the sky is all you've ever seen, can you miss the ground?)
3. What "visions don't depend on outside light"? (Hint: Look up another meaning of *vision*.)
4. Explain "The optic nerve is part of Judgment's eye; Reflected light produces prejudice."
5. How does "blind" differ from "sightless" in the final line? (Hint: "sightless" is meant literally, whereas "blind" is meant figuratively.)
6. Label the rhyming end words in each line to reveal the sonnet's rhyme scheme. Label, for example, lines 1 and 3 with A's, and lines 2 and 4 with B's. Then label lines 5 and 7 with C's, and 6 and 8 with D's, and so on, until you get to the final couplet.

Exercise: Write your own poem about deafness, and how what a person can't hear won't hurt him or her (e.g., things like name calling, curse words, cries of grief). Try to write at least six lines, and copy the sonnet rhythm by limiting each line to 10 syllables, with a rhythm that sounds like this: baBOOM baBOOM baBOOM baBOOM baBOOM. (This rhythm pattern is called *iambic pentameter*.) Count out beats on your desk or on your fingers.

Extension: Trade poems with a partner. Tap out each other's rhythms and circle clunky spots—the syllables that ruin the regularity of the rhythm. Suggest ways to smooth the rhythm either by substituting words with different patterns of accented and unaccented syllables, or by eliminating or adding a word (sometimes adding a simple *and* or *then* can fix a clunky rhythm). Revise, and then meet again to read each other's poems aloud and evaluate the improvements.

Further Extension A: Rewrite a free verse version of your poem about deafness. Compare its power to the rhyming version. Answer the following questions:

1. Which one will have the greatest impact upon, and prove most memorable for, a reader?
2. Which flows better?
3. Which is easier to read aloud?
4. Which one will evoke deeper thoughts for the reader?
5. Which do you like better?

Copyright ©2006 *Writing Success Through Poetry*, Susan L. Lipson. This page may be photocopied or reproduced with permission for student use.

Poetry Prompt 5, continued

After you've answered those questions for yourself, ask a partner the very same questions. Did you judge your work the way your partner did? What have you learned about your own work, and about poetry in general?

Further Extension B: Write an imagery-packed scene from the viewpoint of a person lacking either sight or hearing. For instance, write a description of the beach at sunset as perceived by a blind person. Remember to convey the scene with only nonvisual images, such as the warm sand beneath one's toes, the cawing of seagulls overhead, and so forth. For an extra challenge, make at least one of your descriptions reveal a character's emotional perceptions, as well. For example, the description "The soft cawing of seagulls soothed her ears, so accustomed to the annoying scream of sirens and angry horns" shows that the character is a city dweller, without telling you.

Poetry Prompt 6

Knock, Knock . . . Who's There?

Knock, knock.
A timid tap;
Who's there?
Someone unsure of him- or herself:
My child's shy, little friend;
A self-conscious salesperson, or a
timid new client;
A person who almost wishes I won't
answer the door?

Knock, knockety-knock, knock—
Knock knock!
A rhythmic, musical rap;
Who's there?
Someone playful, driven by inner
music:
A dear friend, announcing herself
through rhythmic familiarity;
A very confident salesperson, or an
eager client;
A person who gets joy out of the
beat, regardless of
whether I answer the door?

KNOCK KNOCK KNOCK
KNOCK!
Rude, insistent banging;

Who's there?
Someone I might not want to see:
An angry neighbor, looking for a fight;
A loud, pushy salesperson, or an over-
eager client;
A person who feels entitled to be
heard, and demands prompt atten-
tion?

KNOCKKNOCKKNOCKKNOCK-
KNOCKKNOCKKNOCK . . .
A stream of desperate pounding;
Who's there?
A troubled friend, an endangered
stranger, or my child with a skinned
knee, seeking help;
A person who's pounding mad that
my doorbell doesn't work;
One who's rude enough to keep
banging, even though he/she knows
that I don't answer the door when
I'm busy writing?

Who's there?
Listen to the knock.
The door might answer you before
you answer the door.

Copyright ©2006 *Writing Success Through Poetry*, Susan L. Lipson. This page may be photocopied or reproduced with permission for student use.

Poetry Prompt 6, continued

For Discussion:

1. What do you notice about the structure of this poem? Examine each stanza, line by line, to see how each line has a specific purpose. For example, each stanza opens with *onomatopoeia* (a word that imitates the sound it represents) that determines the guesses about the knocker's identity that immediately follow that opening line.
2. Which images are repeated from one stanza to another, and why?
3. What does the last line mean? (Hint: Our impressions of people often depend upon the way they dress, act, speak—and even knock.)

Exercise: Focus on a "loaded" sound, which, like a knock—depending on its volume or rhythm—can indicate a lot about the maker of the sound. Thus, the sound you choose should come from a person (or even an animal) with personality. Write your own comparative sound poem, modeled on the above poem. Some sounds to consider: clearing of a throat (ahem!), a laugh, a sniff or snort, a cry, tapping on a desk, honking a horn, answering a phone, playing an instrument, praying, footsteps, and so forth. Make each verse or paragraph (if you choose instead to write prose) show a different manner of expressing the same basic sound. Again, the sound should reveal something about its maker.

Extension: Practice performing your sound-based poem, and then do so. Tape your performance if you can. Did your poem have performable eloquence? In other words, did it make you want to read it aloud and expressively, and did the words flow and touch your listeners in some way? Would another reader be able to recite it your poem the way you did, or does the punctuation and line division need tweaking? Let another reader present your work and note any differences in his or her reading of your poem.

Further Extensions A & B: Another exercise in sound power: Stressing certain words can actually guide the plot of a story. Watch what happens when the exact same dialogue line forms the basis of two completely different written conversations, solely because a different word is emphasized.

Using the dialogue line "Yes, I know you love me . . .," build a conversation, colored with description and action (remember D.A.D.), to fashion a fully imaginable word picture. The given line may appear as the first line of your scene or as the response to a line of dialogue spoken by another character. Before writing the scene, choose one of the five words in the given line to underline for emphasis. The word you choose to emphasize will dictate how your other character responds, and thus, control the scene. You will do this exercise twice, each time choosing a different word to emphasize. For example, two very different scenes

Copyright ©2006 *Writing Success Through Poetry*, Susan L. Lipson. This page may be photocopied or reproduced with permission for student use.

Poetry Prompt 6, continued

could arise from the following lines: "Yes, I know you *love* me . . ." and "Yes, I know *you* love me . . ." The first version, for example, could continue with the words " . . . but do you respect me, too?" The second could be the opening of a complaint from a child to one parent about the other parent neglecting him or her.

Now, write your two different dialogues, featuring the same prompt line, with different emphasized words. You could write these with a partner, or simply read your own pieces aloud with a partner once you have two first drafts. Compare and discuss any similarities or differences in your pieces. Edit each other's work, of course, and revise as needed.

Copyright ©2006 *Writing Success Through Poetry*, Susan L. Lipson. This page may be photocopied or reproduced with permission for student use.

Poetry Prompt 7

Chore, Chore, Forevermore

The girl, with hands in soapsuds, scrubbed with might;
The plates would shine, she set her mind, that night,
For life as Mom's beloved did depend
Upon her dedication to the end,
For without dishes on which they could eat,
The girl would starve, and never have a treat.
Her Dad had said, "We all must earn our keep,"
And thus, the earnest girl vowed not to sleep,
For if her chores were ever left undone,
She'd surely lose the privilege called "fun,"
And never know of "free time" anymore—
Was "slavery" the purpose of this chore?

Poetry Prompt 7, continued

For Discussion:

1. What do you notice about the rhyme scheme of "Chore, Chore, Forevermore"? When two lines, one following the other, use ending words that rhyme, they are called *couplets*.
2. Do you think the girl would really "starve" without clean dishes, or that her mother's love would really depend on her dedication to her chores? Why would a writer exaggerate someone's point of view this way? Look up *hyperbole* in the dictionary and ask yourself whether the poem uses this technique.
3. Would a nonrhyming, free-verse style have suited this topic as well as a rhyming style? Why or why not?
4. Tap out the rhythm of each line. It should sound like this: ba-BUM baBUM baBUM baBUM baBUM. This rhythm pattern has a name, just as the rhyme pattern did. This rhythm pattern is called *iambic pentameter*, which means that each line is composed of five syllable pairs (10 beats total), and each syllable pair is called a *metric foot* (a pentameter equals five metric feet). In this case, it is an iambic foot, consisting of one unaccented syllable followed by an accented syllable (baBUM). Just as in music, poetry has its own terms for rhythms and measures. A poem is simply a song recited or read, rather than sung or heard.

Exercise: Imitate the hyperbolic style of that couplet poem to create your own poem that exaggerates some other task a person might complain about, and show that person's overdramatic point of view in your word choices. Have fun! Maintain the same rhythm in each line.

You may write this with a partner or alone—it is your choice. Clap or tap out (quietly) your rhythms to check for clunky lines or awkward rhymes. Finally, perform your funny poem as though it were a rap song (many rap songs use couplets).

Extension Exercise: Write a humorous, hyperbolic story or poem about a student trying to avoid his parent's discovery of a lousy report card. A high school student used this simile in his story: "I crept past the kitchen doorway like a police officer on a stakeout, avoiding the parental unit stationed at the counter."

Further Extension A: "Chore, Chore, Forevermore" paints a simple picture of a character. Use your own words to paint a more complex character portrait. Start by opening the white pages of a telephone book and randomly placing your finger on someone's name. (If the first choice doesn't inspire you with an image, try up to three selections, and then choose your character's name.) Now open the Yellow Pages of the phone book, and randomly choose a business. This chosen business could be the character's workplace, or a service or product that the character seeks for some reason (e.g., a fence maker—perhaps to keep a bothersome neighbor away—and used furniture, because the character has to

Copyright ©2006 *Writing Success Through Poetry*, Susan L. Lipson. This page may be photocopied or reproduced with permission for student use.

Poetry Prompt 7, continued

move and needs furniture, but can't afford new things). Write a short story or a simple scene consisting of a few paragraphs based on the imaginary information you've gained during your phone book search. Show at least one positive trait of your character and one negative trait to create a truly believable and memorable person for your reader.

Further Extension B: Edit the phone book story after you have spent a day or two away from it, or with an editing partner. Remember to pay attention to content first, and proofread details last. Jot down notes to yourself to guide your revision process, and apply the steps of the editing checklist in Appendix A to your work.

Copyright ©2006 *Writing Success Through Poetry*, Susan L. Lipson. This page may be photocopied or reproduced with permission for student use.

Poetry Prompt 8

Nana's Ring

I didn't want your ring.
Didn't want it?!
This sparkling attractor of eyes
And compliments,
This precious reminder
Of your knotted, but soft, hands,
Too knotted to wear the ring,
And too busy, anyway—
Cooking, wrapping "cheecken" and "latkes"
In petite foil packages for me,
So you'd know I was "eating goot;"
This ring that twinkles silvery blue,
As your eyes once did,
When you locked it up for Someday—
As in: "Someday dis ring vil be yours, Suseleh;"
But I didn't want your ring then,
For I dreaded Someday, then.
And now, as I gaze upon my finger,
Graced by your shining presence,
I smile with misty eyes
And admit that now,
It is some day,
Some wonderful day,
To treasure both intangible and tangible
Memories of you,
And to admit that
I really do want your ring.

Copyright ©2006 *Writing Success Through Poetry*, Susan L. Lipson. This page may be photocopied or reproduced with permission for student use.

Poetry Prompt 8, continued

For Discussion:

1. Why didn't the narrator want the ring? What must happen first for the narrator to get the ring?
2. What does *tangible* mean? What about *intangible*? List five examples of both.
3. Which mean more to you—tangible things or intangible things?
4. Memories often link tangible things with intangible things. Does the intangible feeling of the nervous excitement on the first day of school return when you sharpen new pencils and load brand-new backpacks for school each fall?

Exercise: Think of a tangible item that brings to your mind something intangible, such as love for a person who has passed away, laughter once shared with a best friend, or the warmth of a campfire. Write a poem or a paragraph that shows you with the thing that reminds you of a fond or touching memory. Show yourself handling or viewing the item, and then let the reader peek into your mind to experience the memory that the item brings to your mind.

Extension: Pick a random object from the room (or from a mystery bag of random objects). Invent a reason why it has special value for someone, and then invent the person who values it. Write a prose scene to show the person discovering or rediscovering the object. Show the character's feelings about the intangible qualities of the item through his or her actions and words.

Further Extension A: If the person you invented in the above exercise had positive feelings for the object, rewrite a second version to show the person's negative feelings now (and vice versa, if the original portrayed negative feelings for the object).

Further Extension B: Rewrite yet again, but this time to show your person losing the object, rather than discovering or rediscovering it. Have your character show extreme disappointment over the loss. Which portrayal of the object—its discovery or its loss—has more emotional impact, and why? How could you change one to meet or exceed the impact of the other one?

Copyright ©2006 *Writing Success Through Poetry*, Susan L. Lipson. This page may be photocopied or reproduced with permission for student use.

Poetry Prompt 9

Thirsty Plant and Cloudy Sky*

"Oh Sky, what's wrong? You're looking
awfully blue;
Friend, tell me, is there something I
can do?
Your face is clouded over,
Your expression is quite bleak;
I have noticed this depression,
You've been bottled up all week.
Please Sky, I'm Plant, your friend
who'll share your pain;
Confide in me, and let your teardrops
rain."

"But Plant, dear friend, I do not want
to cry,
Because my tears dim Heaven's
golden eye.
Whenever I start crying,
My tantrums get most stormy;
I roar, and I make such a scene
That you might just abhor me.
And so Plant, please, don't ask to
share my woe,
Believe me, such small pains you need
not know."

"Oh, on the contrary—a friend
should know,
For woe that's shared becomes but
half a woe;
Remember the old saying,
Whenever you want to cry,

That "misery loves company,"
And good company am I.
Now sob, my friend; release a thunderous yell!
Shared tears help friendships grow,
[winking] and ME as well—
truth to tell!"

"What's that you say, sly Plant? Are
you not true?
I hope for friendship's sake I misheard
you.
Perhaps you really meant that you
Are swelled with truth to tell?
[Plant nods, but looks guilty]
Perhaps you are the one who needs
To confide in me, as well.
Oh shame! A friendly offer to so
misconstrue—
Forgive me, for the clouds affect my
view!
[crying, wipes away a "tear" with each
syllable:] Boo hoo!"

[Plant, with palms up to catch the rain.
Aside:] "Phew!"

*A poem suitable for dramatic reading (two parts,
subdivisible for two teams of Plant and Sky readers, with each performer, or pair of performers,
assigned to two lines)

Copyright ©2006 *Writing Success Through Poetry*, Susan L. Lipson. This page may be photocopied or reproduced with permission for student use.

Poetry Prompt 9, continued

For Discussion:

1. What poetic device describes the technique of presenting things as having the qualities of a person?

2. Discuss the relationship between the plant and the sky in this poem. Why does Plant want Sky to cry to him? Does Plant want to comfort his friend, or just to help himself? Is this an open, loving relationship? What behavior would have to change to make this a real friendship?

3. Make a list of new vocabulary words in this poem. The traditional style of the poem lends itself to more formal vocabulary, which is why you see words like *misconstrue*. Look up the new words and jot down their meanings, quoting the poem in your definition, to help you remember the word.

4. Double meanings appear in many spots in this poem to heighten the humor. Find and discuss the two meanings of each these words: *blue, stormy, thunderous,* and *swelled*.

5. What happens when Plant says, "Phew!" at the end of the poem?

Exercise: Brainstorm a list of pairs in nature, like the plant and the sky, that depend upon each other for survival (e.g., trees and roots, flowers and bees). Write your own poetic dialogue (a written conversation in poem form) between one of the pairs on your list. You may use humor or choose a serious tone for your poem.

Extension: Write about a pair of human friends who have a dishonest relationship like that of the Plant and the Sky. Instead of writing just a dialogue, show the relationship between the two through descriptions and actions that reveal their true feelings behind their words. In other words, give the characters words to say, but put more emphasis on emotion-revealing descriptions and actions such as clenched-teeth smiles, sadly slumping shoulders, a concealed smirk, and so forth. Remember, in writing, as in life, actions often speak more loudly than words.

Further Extension A: Fill in this skeletal dialogue with actions (change the dialogue tags also) and description for a vivid word picture:

> "Will you please help me with this?" she asked.
> "Now?" he replied.

Recopy the dialogue lines onto another sheet of paper, leaving enough space between them to fill in the blanks, so to speak. Now elaborate on the dialogue with description and action to reveal (a) the identity of the "this" to which she refers, (b) the tones of voice that show their attitudes toward each other, (c) the context of the dialogue, and (d) who the speakers are.

Copyright ©2006 *Writing Success Through Poetry*, Susan L. Lipson. This page may be photocopied or reproduced with permission for student use.

Poetry Prompt 9, continued

Further Extension B: Do the same exercise you did in Further Extension A, but change the scene entirely with new elaborations. You'll be amazed at how the same dialogue lines, with different descriptions and actions, can produce a very different scene. For example, simply changing "replied" in the second line to "whined" will create a different tone and, possibly, different characters.

Copyright ©2006 *Writing Success Through Poetry*, Susan L. Lipson. This page may be photocopied or reproduced with permission for student use.

Poetry Prompt 10

Life as a Tree: A Song

Oh, how much better off we'd be,
If everyone lived like the tree!
Reaching upward, toward the Light,
Even during the darkest night,
Standing firmly upon our ground,
As each new season comes around;
And valuing our deep, strong roots,
Just as much as our new, green shoots;
Limbs extended, we all embrace
All of the Earth and all in space.
Oh, how much better off we'd be,
If everyone lived like the tree!
Broadening while we're heightening,
Though stormy weather's frightening,
We grow by giving to our Earth,
Showing how much our lives are
worth;
We give far more than we receive,
Living upright until we leave;
We blossom proudly by our peers,
Never hold back because of fears,
Never hold back for pride or shame,
When buds and trunks are not the
same.
Oh, how much better off we'd be,
If everyone lived like the tree!

We dance with earthquakes and in
monsoons,
Branches catching harsh winds as
tunes,
And while they whistle, we conduct,
Waving limbs while our leaves are
plucked,
Yet never bending to snatch them
back—
What's gone is gone, and we don't
lack.
Branching out, we change our view,
And those who climb us see it, too.
Oh, how much better off we'd be,
If everyone lived like the tree!
We offer shelter and food and shade,
And only ask for respect in trade,
And that's how nature's power shows,
And how our awe for our world
grows.
For seeds of goodness connect us all,
And help those tower who might
look small;
We weather seasons so gracefully,
Happy to live life like a tree.
Oh, how much better off we'd be,
If everyone lived like the tree!

Copyright ©2006 *Writing Success Through Poetry*, Susan L. Lipson. This page may be photocopied or reproduced with permission for student use.

Poetry Prompt 10, continued

For Discussion:

1. Notice the rhyme scheme in these song lyrics. When two lines with rhyming end words appear, one after the other, we call them *couplets*. Why do you think couplets often appear in songs? Can you think of a song full of couplets?
2. How is the chorus (repeated lines) of a song similar in literary function to the thesis in an essay?
3. Does this poem use personification? Or, does it do the opposite, making humans sound like trees?
4. Why is "Light" capitalized in the first stanza? Aside from sunlight, what might this mean?
5. What do these phrases have in common: "standing firmly upon our ground," "valuing our deep, strong roots," "living upright," and "branching out, we change our view"? (Hint: Think in terms of double meanings.)
6. Songs often use grammatically incorrect phrases so that when sung, the words sound like common speech. How is "like" used incorrectly in the poem? Would the grammatically correct line "If everyone lived as a tree lives" offer a catchy sound for the chorus? Even if the same line was used, minus "lives," the meaning of the words would alter: "If everyone lived as a tree" implies that we might all turn into trees.

Exercise: Write about another role model from nature: a mountain, the ocean, a flower, an animal, a cloud, the wind, and so forth. List admirable qualities that relate to human behaviors. Use this list to compose a persuasive letter to humanity about why we should all strive to live like your natural role model.

Extension: Rewrite the above exercise as a poem, rhymed or unrhymed.

Further Extension A: Pick another natural element that, in its regular action, describes some aspect of your personality. Write a metaphorical poem that describes you as that element. Title your personification piece "My Life as a _____." Perhaps you're a hot-tempered tornado when angry, sweeping up anyone who gets in your way. Or maybe you're a solid boulder, even when other natural elements (e.g., winds of worry, tears from unhappy skies) attempt to erode you. Maybe you're a turtle, retreating into your shell when you get scared.

Further Extension B: Finish this sentence and substitute the "He or she" with the name of someone you know: "He or she thinks of me like a _____, when in reality, I'm more of a _____." Then, show this misperception of you in a dialogue (don't forget the description and action) between you and that person you know. Show the reader how you're really "more of a _____," but that your friend doesn't recognize your true self. Or, you could have your friend recognize who you really are by the end of the dialogue.

Copyright ©2006 *Writing Success Through Poetry*, Susan L. Lipson. This page may be photocopied or reproduced with permission for student use.

Poetry Prompt 11

Daybreak

Earth, sleeping soundly, dreams of
Spring,
Beneath her blanket, vast and white;
The time for dawn soon comes again,
The pinkish sky is full of light.

The morning Sun warms Earth's numb
bones,
Then peels the blanket from her skin,
And groggy, Earth awakens now,
As Mother Nature calls her kin.

Her plants and trees all stretch their
limbs,
While Sun adds color to Earth's skin,
Then Earth calls, "Mother, water
please,"
And Mother Nature pours some in.

And once parched Earth has
quenched her thirst,
Her face is brilliantly glowing;
She feels so healthy, so alive,
And keeps on growing and growing.

Late in the day, it gets so hot
That hardy Earth becomes afraid
Of drying up and turning brown,
And so, she makes her own cool shade.
Slowly, Earth cools down, relieved,
To fan terrain with leaves that swirl
In chilling winds, which pull them
down,

Toward the ground, where they unfurl.

This active day tires out dear Earth,
She knows it's time to end her day;
Her friend Sun will set early now,
Her friend Sky looks all worn and
gray.

She yawns, and swallows frozen drops
Of water crystallized as flakes;
She shudders as the coldness spreads,
Solidifying ponds and lakes.

Lying still, Earth says her prayers,
And whispers to herself, "Goodnight";
Sky lays the blanket onto her,
While plugging in her moon nightlight.

He kisses Earth with lips of pink,
Streaked across his purplish face;
Earth sighs in peace, now tucked in
tight,
She dreams of grass and Queen
Anne's Lace.

She dreams that flowers will erupt,
Into volcanic Spring, so bright,
That, when at Daybreak, she awakes,
She'll soon forget that wintry Night.

A season passes in that way,
As though it were but one long day.

Copyright ©2006 *Writing Success Through Poetry*, Susan L. Lipson. This page may be photocopied or reproduced with permission for student use.

Poetry Prompt 11, continued

For Discussion:

1. That poem follows a traditional form until the last two-line stanza, which is a couplet. What is the function of the couplet, and to what part of an essay could you compare that function?
2. Analyze each paragraph in terms of the personified symbols and their seasonal counterparts. For example, what is the "blanket" that Sky lays over Earth? Also, look at the rhyme scheme and tap out the rhythms.

Exercise: Choose three stanzas, separate syllable pairs in each line by slashes, and then underline all stressed syllables in each line so you can see the rhythm, as well as hear it. To do this, read the line aloud, and listen to the beats that you naturally emphasize as you read. For example: "As though/it were/but one/long day." Each syllable pair is called a *metric foot* in poetry. You can describe the metric feet in this poem as unstressed/stressed, also known in poetic terms as *iambs*, or *iambic feet*. We speak of poetry's rhythm in terms of its feet and its meter. Thus, we refer to a line of four feet (four syllable pairs), as in "Daybreak," as written in *tetrameter*, and a line of five metric feet (as in Shakespeare's sonnets) as *pentameter*. (One foot = monometer; two feet = dimeter; three feet = trimeter; six feet = hexameter; seven feet = heptameter.)

Once you've labeled three stanza's worth of lines, look at the pattern you've outlined. Notice any irregularities. Often a poem diverges slightly from its pattern for various reasons: (a) the poet might have overlooked an awkward sounding line; (b) the reader might be reading the words differently than the poet would; (c) the off-beat words were simply the best possible words, and the poet chose not to sacrifice meaning for perfect rhythm; or (d) the poet altered the rhythm purposely, to call the reader's attention to a certain word or line. For example, "Streaked across his purplish face" lacks one syllable for this line that should have had four metric feet, and it begins with a stressed syllable, rather than an unstressed one. The second reason above explains the irregularity: forcing readers to elongate the sound of "streaked" makes the word itself seem to streak across the page.

Poets choose words with the same precision that jewelers choose stones for their glittering pieces. Keep that in mind whenever you write anything. Poetic writing can improve any kind of literature with its specific, "showing" words.

Extension: Now, label the rhyme scheme by assigning one letter to each ending word's sound in a stanza. For example, in the first stanza, the ending words are *Spring, white, again*, and *light*. You would write A after Line 1's Spring, B after white, C after again, and another B after light, since both B's rhyme. Label three stanzas to see the pattern. If you start with a certain rhyme scheme, you usually stay with that pattern throughout the poem, unless you diverge purposely to make a point. A perfect example of such divergence is the final couplet in "Daybreak," in which a two line stanza has rhyming end words to conclude the poem by breaking its rhythm and calling the reader's attention to the main point of the poem.

A shorter version of the same poetic idea of "Daybreak" follows.

Copyright ©2006 *Writing Success Through Poetry*, Susan L. Lipson. This page may be photocopied or reproduced with permission for student use.

Poetry Prompt 11, continued

A Seasonal Day

Our seasons form a metaphor,
A year boiled down to one long day,
From warm sunrise to cool sunset,
From Spring's blue sky to Winter's gray;
A day that starts in flowery May,
With lunchtime picnics in July,
And after lunch, November's chill
Makes vivid leaves fall down and die.
Then Winter comes to tuck Earth in
Beneath a blanket, soft and white,
Where Earth then sleeps till dawn creeps up
To chase away the dark with light.
Once Earth has warmed her stiffened limbs
The year-day can begin anew,
The blanket melts away and up,
Forms puffs of cotton in sky blue;
The cotton balls soaked in old snow
Soon leak and gush on Earth's dry face;
Her wrinkles and her dry spots fade—
Brown crevices become green space.
And so go days for dear old Earth,
Who never fears the long day's end,
Who treasures both the dawn and dusk,
For she sees each day as a trend.

Copyright ©2006 *Writing Success Through Poetry*, Susan L. Lipson. This page may be photocopied or reproduced with permission for student use.

Poetry Prompt 11, continued

For Discussion:

1. Do you prefer one poem to the other, and if so, why?
2. What are the strengths and weaknesses of each version?

Further Extension A: Highlight three examples of personification in either "Daybreak" or "A Seasonal Day." Why do you think many illustrators like to illustrate pieces that include personification? Illustrate one of the personification examples yourself, and then answer that question.

Further Extension B: Express the following lines in personified terms, and make sure to stimulate two or more senses for your reader. For instance, "The beautiful autumn leaves covered the ground as we hiked through them along the path" could become "The trees had laid down a dense, crisp carpet of sunset colors to soften the thuds of our hiking boots as we entered their tranquil home."

1. The hikers entered the cave. (Try making the cave your personified subject.)
2. The trees sway gently in the wind. (This offers a natural place for a simile.)
3. Raindrops hit the windows. (How hard, how loudly? Choose a showing verb.)

Choose your favorite revision of the above three, and turn it into a poem of any style.

Copyright ©2006 *Writing Success Through Poetry*, Susan L. Lipson. This page may be photocopied or reproduced with permission for student use.

Poetry Prompt 12

A Fly That Tried

I insulted a fly today.
When I heard him buzzing around me
and felt him land on my arm,
at first my heart sped up a bit
at the thought that he was a bee;
But then I looked at him and sighed,
"Phew! Only a fly!"
So I shooed him off my arm.
I could have sworn I heard him buzz,
"I don't get no respect!"
as he flew away,
daydreaming about growing a stinger.

Copyright ©2006 *Writing Success Through Poetry*, Susan L. Lipson. This page may be photocopied or reproduced with permission for student use.

Poetry Prompt 12, continued

For Discussion:

1. Is this poem traditional or free verse?
2. How would you summarize the main point of this poem?
3. What verb shows personification of the fly?
4. Why does the fly want a stinger?
5. Have you ever wished that you looked different so you could gain more respect?

Exercise: Show how you would react to a spider on your bedroom floor. You may write a poem like the one above, or simply a prose paragraph. You could show yourself imagining the spider talking to you, or you could make the spider actually talk, creating a piece in the fantasy genre. Here is a possible opening line for you: I spotted a silvery spider on my rug. Notice the alliteration in the suggested opening line. See if you can work in some alliteration as you write.

Extension: In a paragraph or two, write someone else's reaction to a spider on his or her floor. Show the person as insensitive to fellow creatures through his or her actions. Do not merely tell that he is insensitive. Include facial expressions and body language, as well. For example, does your character cringe at the sight of the spider, wrinkle up her face into a grimace, or back away? You could even add another human character to the scene to react to your main character's actions. Sometimes adding other characters helps to develop your main character even further through the eyes of others.

Further Extension A: Take the same spider and put it in the room of a nature lover. Write the new scene, showing the new character's humane treatment of the spider, and thus, revealing the gentleness of his or her personality. Remember to let your readers see, hear, and touch something along with your character in the scene.

Further Extension B: Think of a physical quality you've wished you had, and write about what happens when you suddenly find yourself with that quality. You look different to others; will they notice and respect you more? Will you have to make them notice? What happens when they do notice? Do you gain new friends? Are they real friends? Show this scene in two to three paragraphs.

Copyright ©2006 *Writing Success Through Poetry*, Susan L. Lipson. This page may be photocopied or reproduced with permission for student use.

Poetry Prompt 13

Home Is Where You Are

Don't fall in love with a place too much,
Because places often change.
Don't fall in love with a home you have,
Because homes can be rearranged.
For as long as you have someone whom you love,
To hold in your arms,
It's after you cross the threshold together
That a house takes on its charms—
It's the people who wear its charms.

Don't pine away over leaving home,
Because home is where you are.
Your home, like you is a mobile thing;
You can follow it in you car.
Just remember a house does not become "home,"
Till there is love inside;
It's after you cross the threshold together
That a house inspires your pride—
Home's the people who live inside.

Copyright ©2006 *Writing Success Through Poetry*, Susan L. Lipson. This page may be photocopied or reproduced with permission for student use.

Poetry Prompt 13, continued

For Discussion:

1. Can you tell that this poem is actually a song lyric? What clues indicate that it's a song?
2. What do you know about the narrator of these words? To whom might the advice be addressed?
3. Do you agree with the narrator's words? Is a house different from a home? How?

Exercise: Write a multisensory description of a room in your own home. Show the reader not only how it looks (e.g., perhaps the room has yellow walls, hanging shelves full of cookbooks, and a candlestick collection), but also what sounds one might hear while visiting the room (e.g., the sizzle of vegetables in a pan, the bickering of young siblings, a piano playing Beethoven), and/or what smells, textures, or physical sensations one might encounter (e.g., the scent of cinnamon potpourri, the downy softness of a thick bedspread, or the gentle, undulating breeze of a ceiling fan).

Extension: Ask a reader to experience a trip to your room via your words from the above exercise. Ask your reader the following questions:

1. Did I show you my room, rather than simply tell you about it?
2. If some passages merely tell, will you write "Please show" over those lines?
3. Did my description of the room reveal anything about me, in particular?
4. If the description revealed nothing specific about me, how would you recommend that I do so?

Use the reader's answers to aid your revision. Ask the reader to reread the next draft.

Further Extension A: Write a description of a room—specifically, the belongings in that room—to show the personality of your favorite fictitious character. For example, Harry Potter's room might contain a wand shelf hanging just beside his bed, a broomstick stand, a closet full of black cloaks, a trophy for Quidditch expertise, and magically moving birthday cards from his friends. Trade room descriptions with another student, and guess the identity of each room's inhabitant.

Further Extension B: Write a poem of contrasts in two columns. One column features a list of items beginning with the words "A house is . . ." and the second list consists of lines that complete the phrase "But a home is . . ."

Copyright ©2006 *Writing Success Through Poetry*, Susan L. Lipson. This page may be photocopied or reproduced with permission for student use.

Poetry Prompt 14

Buried Dreams

I dug a hole,
and when it was deep,
I piled my dreams
in a tear-soaked heap.

Into the pit,
Like rotting, old wood,
I hid each log,
as well as I could.

Tried to forget
what kindling was for,

Gave up on fire—
all plans I'd ignore.

I walked away . . .
but soon stopped, in pain,
Then ran to dig
my dreams up again!

With aching arms,
I set them aglow,
fanned faithful flames . . .
Now dreams—and I—grow.

Copyright ©2006 *Writing Success Through Poetry*, Susan L. Lipson. This page may be photocopied or reproduced with permission for student use.

Poetry Prompt 14, continued

For Discussion:

1. This poem compares the act of giving up on dreams with the act of discarding usable firewood. Yet, the poem does not make this comparison in an obvious way by using like or as, but, rather, by using a metaphor, a figurative comparison that is not as obvious as a simile. A metaphor does not directly show similarities, but rather suggests those similarities indirectly and symbolically. What does "the fire" symbolize?
2. How would this poem affect you if it used no rhyme or rhythm?
3. Count the syllables in each line and note the number by each line. Do you see the pattern?
4. This poetic style is called *light verse*, and this poem ends with a universal message. State the message in your own words.

Exercise: Look up the poet Langston Hughes, and find his poem "Dreams" ("Hold fast to dreams/ For if dreams die/ Life is a broken-winged bird/ That cannot fly . . ."). Write your own metaphor about the importance of our personal dreams, in imitation of either the light style of "Buried Dreams" or the serious style of the poem by Hughes.

Extension: Write a short story about a person temporarily discarding a lifelong dream, only to realize that the dream has too much value to throw away. Start by picking the dream and the dreamer (main character). Then, decide what frustrating event led to the character's desire to walk away from his or her dreams in the first place. Show, don't tell, as you write, using specific details and the D.A.D. technique to paint your scene. Also, keep in mind the M.O.M. technique. Choose words that show a definite mood change from start to finish, order your details in a way that shows the change in the character from start to finish, and select only details that matter to the idea of the discarded dream found again.

Further Extension A: Losing something of value—even if we did lose it on purpose—offers us the opportunity for personal growth. What adjective, describing the flames, reflects the idea of personal growth? And, what does the use of that adjective imply about the attitude of a person dedicated to personal growth? Write answers to those questions, and illustrate your answers with quotations from the poem itself as support for your points. Try adding a topic sentence that you will insert before your other sentences to introduce the theme of your paragraph. Then, add a concluding sentence that relates to the topic sentence in a more general way (e.g., "Thus, like the narrator of the poem, we learn that . . . "). See Appendix E for a full outline of one commonly used essay format.

Further Extension B: Add another body paragraph, connected by a transition, to come before the one you wrote in Further Extension A,

Copyright ©2006 *Writing Success Through Poetry*, Susan L. Lipson. This page may be photocopied or reproduced with permission for student use.

Poetry Prompt 14, continued

about faith in our dreams. Pretend you are writing a full Response to Literature Essay (see Appendix E) to "Buried Dreams." One paragraph should flow naturally into the other, and a useful way to create a flowing transition is to repeat words from the previous concluding sentence when writing the topic sentence of the following paragraph. The theme of this additional paragraph should illustrate the struggle we sometimes must endure to keep pursuing our dreams. Start by finding a concrete detail (or C.D.)—a line to quote from the poem—that best illustrates that pursuing dreams is no easy feat. Use the standard body paragraph format again, and include two lines of commentary—one to explain the C.D., and the other to offer your analysis, or interpretation of what you explained. Remember to build upon the C.D. Finish the paragraph with a topic sentence and a concluding sentence. Read this paragraph, and the one now connected to it, to a classmate or teacher for feedback. Take notes about any editorial comments you receive, and revise accordingly. Try writing an introductory paragraph and a concluding paragraph, thus forming a four-paragraph Response to Literature essay.

Copyright ©2006 *Writing Success Through Poetry*, Susan L. Lipson. This page may be photocopied or reproduced with permission for student use.

Poetry Prompt 15

Flew the Coop

You mistook me for a pigeon—
trainable, with an instinctive
homing device—
and attempted to own me.

But Eagles soar like freed kites,
answering to no tugs,
and returning for no pigeon's
mundane false rewards.

I'm history!
And I won't repeat myself.

Copyright ©2006 *Writing Success Through Poetry*, Susan L. Lipson. This page may be photocopied or reproduced with permission for student use.

Poetry Prompt 15, continued

For Discussion:

1. Who is "you" in the above poem? What do we know about "you" and the relationship between him or her and the narrator?
2. How are pigeons like kites still attached to their string and their controllers? How are eagles more like freed kites?
3. What mood does this poem reflect?
4. What does *mundane* mean? Why are the pigeon's mundane rewards "false"?
5. "I'm history!" is a colloquial American expression. If you haven't heard that expression, it's synonymous to "good-bye and I'm glad to get out of here." What does the last line mean? (Hint: We talk about history repeating itself, especially in war time, and humans make the same mistakes over and over again.)

Exercise: Have you ever heard a friend say, "I won't be your friend if you're friends with her [or him]"? Perhaps a controlling person has always tried to get his or her way in your relationship and you finally got fed up with always having to give in to that person. Rewrite the metaphor from the above poem in plain language in a speech from the person who finally decides to speak out to his or her controlling friend and assert his or her own need for freedom. Give names to the troubled pair.

Extension: Now write a response to the speech from the above exercise from the controlling friend. Add description and actions to your dialogue for a vivid word picture. How will your scene end—tearfully, explosively, quietly? Let your reader feel like an invisible spy in the scene.

Further Extension A: Write a list of three to five similes for the feeling of being controlled by someone. Now write a list of three to five similes for the feeling of being free from someone's control.

Further Extension B: Turn two contrasting similes from the above exercise into your own poem about breaking free from the bonds of an unhealthy relationship.

Copyright ©2006 *Writing Success Through Poetry*, Susan L. Lipson. This page may be photocopied or reproduced with permission for student use.

Poetry Prompt 16

Pen-Pal

My best friend's empathy
is so unbounded
that she takes on,
actually takes on,
my emotions as I share them;
she's one whom I'm never afraid to
be open with
because she never blabs
what I've shared in confidence;
she accepts my feelings readily
as part of her existence,
and never rebukes them;
and she has always been available
when I've needed a friend;
She relieves me of anxieties,
sadness, or fear,
hearing my words
via ink waves (not sound waves)
with fibrous, white ears.

She enables me to make my mark
upon society, upon her, upon the future.
I'm thankful that she
can absorb my words,
this friend of friends—
this paper.

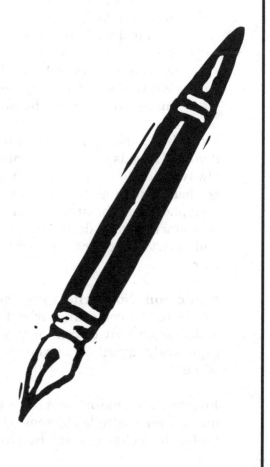

Copyright ©2006 *Writing Success Through Poetry*, Susan L. Lipson. This page may be photocopied or reproduced with permission for student use.

Poetry Prompt 16, continued

For Discussion:

1. How long did it take you to figure out the identity of the best friend? Or, did you only know at the end of the poem?
2. Is this poem really about the paper itself? What must one *first* have for a friendship with paper?

Exercise: Getting one's feelings and thoughts onto paper can bring relief to many writers. Describe a time when you used writing as a way to calm yourself down or get over some painful emotion. Set the scene by showing briefly what event prompted you to write out your frustration, fear, sadness, or longing. You need not include what you actually wrote, only how you did it (show the setting, your mood, your reaction to your words once the flow stopped and you reread, and so forth). Keep this piece as a reminder to you about how much writing can help you cope with life.

Extension: What do you seek in a real best friend—what qualities, capabilities, and moral values? Write a mock want ad, describing in as few words as possible the best friend you seek. When you place an actual advertisement, you pay per word to the newspaper, so you have to make every word count. Keep this economy of words in mind as you write your advertisement.

Further Extension A: Write a response in the form of a business letter to your want ad for a best friend, as if you are the applicant for the job. For each qualification mentioned in the ad, give the advertiser concrete examples of how you fit the description. This is comparable to replacing telling words (like the ones you used in the want ad) with showing examples, as you should do for any piece of writing.

Further Extension B: Imagine meeting the person who replied to your ad in the letter above. Does the person immediately click with you, fulfilling all of your expectations? Or, does the person seem to have lied about certain qualities, revealing that he or she is not really as perfect for you as the letter claimed?

Write a scene using dialogue colored with description and action (D.A.D.) to show your first meeting with this possible best friend. Limit yourself to no more than two pages. Show both actions and reactions to give your reader an idea about what you looked for in this possible best friend and how the new person seemed to you. Edit the scene a week later, after time has sharpened your editorial eye.

Copyright ©2006 *Writing Success Through Poetry*, Susan L. Lipson. This page may be photocopied or reproduced with permission for student use.

Poetry Prompt 17

Aerial View of a Charred Neighborhood (San Diego, 10/28/03)

Rows of former family room fireplaces
Stand like headstones
For homes,
Amid smoking phantom walls,
Against which sofas stood,
Only hours ago.
Their useless chimneys only mark
The remains of the "replaceables,"
While the "irreplaceables"
Cry quietly on camera,
Overwhelmed by their sudden homelessness,
Yet not overcome:
"At least we're all together and safe,"
I hear them say to the reporters,
Over and over, from channel to channel.
"We're all okay, that's all that really matters."

Copyright ©2006 *Writing Success Through Poetry*, Susan L. Lipson. This page may be photocopied or reproduced with permission for student use.

Poetry Prompt 17, continued

For Discussion:

1. Do you remember hearing or reading about the firestorms of 2003 in Southern California, which scarred thousands of acres and burned up entire neighborhoods? Can you picture this scene?
2. Find examples of the following literary techniques in the poem: simile, multisensory imagery, and alliteration.
3. In your opinion, what is the theme of this poem?
4. What are the "replaceables"? What are the "irreplaceables"?

Exercise: Remember or imagine the worst disaster scene you can picture. Write a multisensory poem or prose piece to capture the event as your own personal historical record. Avoid gory details; you want to move readers, not disgust them. Read the piece aloud until you feel sure that it conveys what you see, hear, feel, smell, or taste.

Extension: Look up two or three actual news stories about a famous disaster. Try to find examples of showing writing and figurative language within descriptions of the event. Record the most touching words you find. Then analyze those words for subtle insertions of the writer's point of view. Decide whether the writer showed a balanced account of the story or a biased (one-sided) perspective. If the author wrote an editorial or personal opinion article, then the inclusion of his or her point of view is acceptable and expected. But, if the article purports to be a news story, then the writer must stick to the facts, no matter how vivid the writing style. Record some notes about what you have learned from this exercise.

Further Extensions A & B: A view of a charred neighborhood leaves an indelible image in one's mind. Write a prose piece (1–2 paragraphs) beginning with this sentence: *I've had some trouble putting it out of my mind.* Show what "it" is, who the narrator is, and use both the D.A.D. and M.O.M. elements to create a three-dimensional kind of scene. The "it" need not be a disaster scene. "It" may be a fight with a friend or family member, an anxiety-producing event, and so forth.

Give your first draft to another reader, and ask the reader to read your work aloud to you. Note any changes you need to make based on what you heard. Ask your reader what kind of mood your piece conveyed to him or her. Revise and reread the second draft to the same reader—this time with you reading aloud—and ask for his or her written comments. Finally, add to the reader's written comments your own written observations about the improvement of your piece from the first to the second draft.

Copyright ©2006 *Writing Success Through Poetry*, Susan L. Lipson. This page may be photocopied or reproduced with permission for student use.

Poetry Prompt 18

Free as a Bird

"Free as a bird,"
he croons,
"free as a bird ..."
Oh, that he could be as free as a bird!
He's wishing,
wishing,
wishing that he were;
He needs to soar,
envies the wings,
longs for the flight,
pines for the rush of air,
but
he's clipped his own wings
by feeling their absence,
by wishing, needing, envying, longing, pining,
instead of taking to the wind
in a leap of faith
and becoming,
becoming,
becoming
free
like a bird.

Freedom sought
is freedom found.

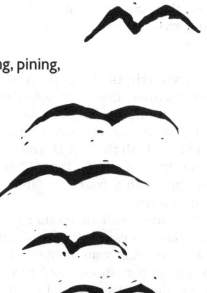

Copyright ©2006 *Writing Success Through Poetry*, Susan L. Lipson. This page may be photocopied or reproduced with permission for student use.

Poetry Prompt 18, continued

For Discussion:

1. The title is purposely *trite* (overused; unoriginal). Why? Could it have to do with the boy's lack of depth in what he desires in life?
2. How does the title imply that "he" seeks freedom just because everyone else does, that he seeks it just to be a "seeker," not really to find freedom?
3. Which words are repeated and why? Repetition, you see, used sparingly, acts to emphasize a word or call attention to its relationship with other repeated words.
4. What is the relationship between "wishing" and "becoming"? Compare it to the relationship between vivid, active verbs and vague, passive verbs (e.g., the active "launches" and the passive "goes").
5. What do these lines mean: "He's clipped his own wings/ by feeling their absence"? Hint: Have you ever heard of self-fulfilling prophecies?
6. Ponder and explain the final two lines. Is the idea reminiscent of something you've heard before?
7. Why was space left between "like a bird" and "Freedom sought"? Do you see how the final two lines differ from the rest of the poem? If this were a fable, what part would those final lines be?

Exercise: Write your own poem titled "As _____ as _____." Some suggestions: "As Bad as They Come," "As Good as Gold," "As Heavy as a Rock," "As Quiet as a Mouse," "As Bright as the Sun" (with *bright* referring either to light or intelligence), and so forth. If you use the technique of irony for humorous effect, make your descriptions clearly reflect the opposite of what the reader would expect to perceive. Make your last two lines sum up your lesson or theme, as the poem on page 72 does.

Extension: Whenever possible, substitute active verbs for passive verbs such as am, is, are, was, were, be, being, been, has, have, had, do, does, and did. Below, a passive paragraph needs your cutting and revising with new verbs (reorder sentences, too, as you wish). Also pay attention to lines that tell but do not show the scene in sensory images (imagery). Rewrite the paragraph to create a vivid word picture without superfluous words.

> There were a lot of kids in the lunch area when the emergency bell rang. The emergency bell was ringing and the kids were leaving the area to protect themselves in the auditorium. BRRRING, BRRRING, BRRRING! There was an adult's voice talking to everyone on the loudspeaker telling kids not to panic, but they did. The auditorium was a scene of chaos.

Copyright ©2006 *Writing Success Through Poetry*, Susan L. Lipson. This page may be photocopied or reproduced with permission for student use.

Poetry Prompt 18, continued

Further Extension A: Experiment with the relative power of verbs. Copy the sentence below, which features a "blah" verb much like the passive verbs above, and change the verb at least 10 times to change the scene and/or the character. Note the possible perceptions of the reader with each different verb.

> Trevor went around the yard.

For example: With *crawled* as the verb, Trevor might become a baby, or a person searching for something in the grass. With *staggered*, Trevor might have been injured.

Further Extension B: "Blah" verbs, like *went*, merely tell the reader what the author wants the reader to experience. "Blah" verbs fail to show what is happening—which is our aim in creating vivid word pictures. Review the list of adjectives and verbs to avoid whenever possible, and then add at least 10 more of your own.

Adjectives and Verbs to Avoid Whenever Possible in Narration

said	looked	pretty	colorful
did	ugly	cool	funny
moved	beautiful	little	big
went	nice	old	interesting
looked	different	young	odd
has	unique	handsome	cute

You may want to play a game with two or more other writers, or with your whole class. Use description, action, and dialogue (D.A.D.) to "paint" one of the words from the list above. When you write your D.A.D. paragraph, have at least one classmate try to guess what telling word you are trying to show. Discuss which guesses fit, and which do not, and analyze why. Revise the paragraph as necessary, to help the reader understand what images you wish to convey.

Copyright ©2006 *Writing Success Through Poetry*, Susan L. Lipson. This page may be photocopied or reproduced with permission for student use.

Poetry Prompt 19

Inspired Rain

And thus it rains
And rains
And rains
It taps the panes
The panes
The panes
It builds its rhythm slowly now
Then faster, faster, faster till it's
Clicking, plinking, plunking now, with
Watery, rippling fingers, it's typing and typing
So frantically typing on keys of glass without ever stopping
To linger to think to revise or to sort—the thoughts keep flowing
While fingers keep typing and typing and typing and typing
Typing a poem about the rain
It types and types like a writer inspired
And after it bangs out the loudest, most polysyllabic, most soundly in-
spired line of all . . .
It wanes, and wanes, and wanes, and wanes and
Finally, finally, stops
To click
Save.

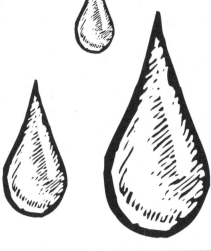

Copyright ©2006 *Writing Success Through Poetry*, Susan L. Lipson. This page may be photocopied or reproduced with permission for student use.

Poetry Prompt 19, continued

For Discussion:

1. Clap out the syllables as you chant this poem aloud. What do you notice about the rhythm? Treat the ellipsis points (the "dot-dot-dot") at the end of the first verse as a pause before continuing to clap out the closing verse.

2. Find one example of personification.

3. What is the metaphor for the rain? How is the rain "like a writer inspired"?

4. How is the inspiration to write a poem like a rainstorm?

5. What double meaning can you see in the last four words: "stops / to click / Save"?

Exercise: Write a poem to show a sound via a simile or metaphor that calls the sound to one's mind—such as typing, which calls to mind the pattering of raindrops. Use rhythm, repetition, and/or rhyme to heighten the sensory image, as the carefully measured lines do above. Consider sounds such as: windshield wipers, drum beats, a crowd cheering, bicycle pedaling, skateboarding, sprinklers, tap dancing, marching, and so forth.

Extension: Write a poem or short prose piece (2–3 paragraphs) that begins (and maybe even ends, too), with this line: "I can still hear its echo today. . . ." Pick a sound image that is very memorable for many reasons, and let your reader experience that memorable image through the details you show.

Further Extension A: If you wrote a poem for the extension lesson above, turn it into prose now, or vice versa. Compare the two pieces and decide which you prefer, and why.

Further Extension B: Write your reasons for preferring either the prose or the poetry form of the same prompt, and comment on your preference in terms of the power of your words within each format. For example, did you force your words into a poetic structure and thus hinder your message? Or, did the prose lack the power of the short rhythmically designed lines of your poem, which enhanced the message with its form?

Copyright ©2006 *Writing Success Through Poetry*, Susan L. Lipson. This page may be photocopied or reproduced with permission for student use.

Poetry Prompt 20

Neighborly Love

In ancient days, no doors were ever locked;
And silversmiths had not invented keys;
If Man had visitors, they never knocked,
For loving neighbors made him feel at ease.
And then one day Man found his home was robbed;
Some thief had emptied all his walls and floors;
When neighbors heard, the silversmiths were mobbed—
The whole town asked for locks to bar their doors.
They left for church each Sunday with their keys,
To listen to the teachings of their Lord,
And "Love thy neighbor" had been one of these;
They'd seen it in their Bibles, locked and stored.
Now when a neighbor visits Man he knocks,
For what makes loving neighbors but good locks?

Copyright ©2006 *Writing Success Through Poetry*, Susan L. Lipson. This page may be photocopied or reproduced with permission for student use.

Poetry Prompt 20, continued

For Discussion:

1. Contrast the above poem with the thematically similar one that follows, in terms of the literary elements and techniques that define poetry: (a) rhythm and form, (b) performable eloquence, (c) evocative language, (d) figurative expressions, and (e) repetitive sounds. Note your findings as part of a group discussion, if possible.

2. Do you prefer one poem over the other, and why? (Note: Writing exercises appear after "The Key to Society.")

The Key to Society

A symbol of human suspicion—
home owners,
car owners,
bike owners,
store owners,
all owners everywhere
must have a key;
we wouldn't want to get ripped off,
now would we?
Can't trust anyone these days,
so we lock up to be safe
with that guarded piece of metal,
probably invented by the first paranoid mind,
and now a universal possession
in civilized societies.
Just think how much lighter our pockets and hearts would be,
and how we'd never get locked out of our homes,
or our car
or our neighbors' abodes,
if primitive man had not chosen to be
a social animal.

Copyright ©2006 *Writing Success Through Poetry*, Susan L. Lipson. This page may be photocopied or reproduced with permission for student use.

Poetry Prompt 20, continued

Exercise: Pick a boundary or possession marker, such as the key, that has potential for social commentary. Possible choices could be fences, lockers, alarms, white lines to stand behind at the bank, bike locks, curtains, and so forth. Write your own social commentary poem in imitation of the style of "The Key to Society."

Extension: Convert your poem into an Elizabethan-style sonnet, like "Neighborly Love," with 14 lines, every other line rhyming, and the rhythmic pattern called *iambic pentameter* (baBUM baBUM baBUM baBUM baBUM) for each 10 syllable line. One rule to follow: Decide what you want to say first, and then fit your idea into a poetic form. Don't force rhymes that sound silly or unnatural just because they rhyme; instead, find a new rhyming word, or change the previous line to create a whole new rhyme. Forced-sounding rhymes make readers cringe. For example:

> The trees reach out to touch the graying sky,
> With leafless limbs that birds just fly by.

The clunky rhythm and the forced rhyme in the second line stop this poem before it starts. A rhythm and rhyme adjustment could help:

> The trees reach out to touch the graying sky,
> With leafless limbs through which the Fall winds sigh.

Do you hear the difference? Clap out the lines if it helps, a soft clap followed by a harder clap (clapCLAP, clapCLAP . . .).

Further Extension A: "Neighborly Love" and "The Key to Society" both employ the writer's tool of irony—saying the opposite of what one means to make a humorous, though sometimes dark, point about some issue. Irony often uses puns to make points, too. Write a short story, using an ironic tone to maintain a sense of humor in the face of near-tragedy. Read the prompt below:

John's birthday party ends up ruined when someone knocks over the cake and its burning candles, causing a fire and forcing all the party guests to run outside. A possible title could be "A Very Un-Cool Birthday Party." You may find it easier to write as though *you* are John, from his point of view. Have fun with puns and sarcasm—two methods of creating an ironic tone.

Further Extension B: Rewrite the story about John's birthday party as a news report, without humor or any obvious point of view. Remember to cover these journalistic guidelines: who, what, when, where, why, and how. Those six points must appear within the first two paragraphs.

Copyright ©2006 *Writing Success Through Poetry*, Susan L. Lipson. This page may be photocopied or reproduced with permission for student use.

Poetry Prompt 21

A New Mansion

I heard the door slam shut
behind me.
It sent shivers through my body.
But the claustrophobia
that I feared would develop
hadn't even time to become imminent;
For another door burst open
in front of me,
illuminating a new corridor to enter
and many doors yet to open.

Copyright ©2006 *Writing Success Through Poetry*, Susan L. Lipson. This page may be photocopied or reproduced with permission for student use.

Poetry Prompt 21, continued

For Discussion:

1. What do the "mansion" and the "door" represent? What is the "claustrophobia," in metaphorical terms?
2. What emotions appear in this poem?
3. Is this poem about endings, beginnings, or both? Can you relate to the feeling of such a dramatic life-changing event in your own life?
4. How could you explain this as a poem about relationships?

Exercise: Write a paragraph or two about a time when you experienced some dramatic ending in your life—losing a friendship, having to move from your home, the break-up of a family, having to give up some activity or class, graduation, and so forth. Show not only the experience, but also your emotional reaction. If you, like the poem's narrator, experienced a realization about the positive possibilities that came out of your loss, show that, too. For example, perhaps you lost one friend, only to gain another. Or, perhaps you moved from one home, only to find that your new home had even more to offer. In any case, portray the feeling of simultaneous fear and excitement upon this change in your life.

Extension: The following poem written by Masahide appears on a refrigerator magnet:

> Barn's burnt down . . . now I can see the moon.

Such power in just nine words. What positive human quality do both "A New Mansion" and Masahide's poem represent? Write a brief poem like Masahide's, substituting the barn's burning for some other loss, and the new chance to see the moon for some other unforeseen opportunity.

Further Extension A: Edit the following personal prose narrative about a life-changing experience. Focus only on content and stylistic issues (what is said, and how it is expressed). You should focus on editing the paragraph, not just proofreading. Remember, proofreading is not editing for substance.

Edit the author's use of superfluous (unnecessary) words by drawing a single line through those words and marking them "spf." Write "show, don't tell" by words that merely tell the reader about an experience, without involving him or her in the scene. Write "vague" over words that need specific examples, and point out problems in logical flow. Help the author see how to improve and condense the work (making every word count). You do not need to rewrite the piece, only edit (critique) it. Offer helpful direction, not your own words. You could add a comment related to the substance, such as: "Start the story with the first real action: the public announcement about the narrator's crush on a guy."

> One day my best friend told everyone which guy I liked,
> Tyler, after I had asked her never to tell anyone. She

Copyright ©2006 *Writing Success Through Poetry*, Susan L. Lipson. This page may be photocopied or reproduced with permission for student use.

announced that I liked Tyler while we were standing with our usual crowd outside. The worst part was that Tyler was there at the time, and he looked like he was feeling really embarrassed. When I saw his expression, I felt even worse. Then, I acted like a total idiot, and ran away and hid in the empty multipurpose room. I was trying to figure out a good place to hide, where no one could hear how upset I was, and then I went through the double doors super fast and ran up the stage steps to hide behind the stage curtain in the multipurpose room. I sat down hard and began to cry. Just then, Tyler came in. I heard footsteps entering the multipurpose room, and then climbing the steps. When the curtain was pulled back there was Tyler, standing there. I immediately stopped crying and tried to hide my tears. Tyler came and comforted me. I must have looked totally shocked—and thrilled!—when he put his hand on my shoulder and said he hoped I was OK.

Further Extension B: Rewrite the above narrative, as you see it. Show, don't tell.

Copyright ©2006 *Writing Success Through Poetry*, Susan L. Lipson. This page may be photocopied or reproduced with permission for student use.

Poetry Prompt 22

Molten Mind on Ice

An energy eruption—
spurting forth sporadically,
fighting to flow freely,
involuntarily involuntary in its functions.
Constrained conservation—
harnessing, holding, and hiding,
till the time for tapping;
rich resource reserves
grow and grow and grow.
A spirit's cellar—
fully stored with foodstuffs for future seasons;
while hinges hinge on unhinging,
so that foods for thoughts
may force themselves forward,
as a vivid volcano of verbs and vowels—
stunning subjects,
outstanding objects,
moving words to move worlds
outside my own.

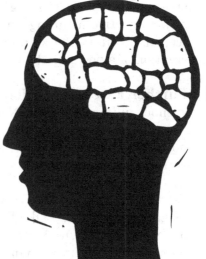

Copyright ©2006 *Writing Success Through Poetry*, Susan L. Lipson. This page may be photocopied or reproduced with permission for student use.

Poetry Prompt 22, continued

For Discussion:

1. What pattern do you see in this poem? (Hint: Underline the repeated beginning consonant sounds in each line.)
2. Look up *alliteration*, if you don't already know what it means. How does alliteration affect the way we hear poems?
3. What other qualities of a poem does this poem possess?
4. Look up any words or phrases you don't know, and then note their definitions. Reread the poem aloud.
5. Do you see how this poem is about a writer bursting with inspiration ("rich resource reserves/ grow and grow and grow")? To what is the writer's overflowing mind compared?
6. Have you ever felt this full of ideas? Does the narrator sound excited with inspiration, or frustrated, or both? Why?
7. How do you know when it's "time for tapping" your thoughts and allowing them to flow onto paper?
8. Explain the play on words in the line: "moving words to move worlds."
9. Think about the title "Molten Mind on Ice." What happens when we put something "on ice"? Why is the narrator trying to cool off her burning inspirations?

Exercise: Experiment with your own alliterations by writing a poem to express either fury or great excitement. Keep your lines short to minimize the numbers of alliterative words you need to find and make flow. Don't force words to fit if they don't sound natural. "Molten Mind on Ice" changed the beginning letters on certain lines when the alliteration didn't allow for logical phrases; remember, nonsense for the sake of sound does not make a good poem.

Extension: Write a poem called "Stirring Words" (address the two possible meanings of "stirring": (a) as a verb meaning "mixing," and (b) as an adjective meaning "moving, or touching." As in "Molten Mind on Ice," use alliteration as much as possible, and show the metaphorical creation of a poem as the poet "stirs a poetic pot," so to speak.

Further Extension A: Rewrite either of the poems you have created without alliteration now. Note the differences as you read them aloud, either to yourself, onto a tape recording, or to another person. Record notes about your observations regarding the effects of alliteration on both the meaning and the sound of a poem.

Further Extension B: Find examples of alliteration in newspaper and magazine headlines and ads. Cut them out and arrange them on blank paper into your own "Alliteration Gallery." Why do media writers use alliteration? To create memorable lines for readers who also happen to be consumers? To draw the reader's eyes and ears to a certain article? Simply to amuse themselves with their own clever word choices and word plays? Analyze each clipping you've collected and consider which reason for using alliteration seems to apply to each example. Make notes.

Copyright ©2006 *Writing Success Through Poetry*, Susan L. Lipson. This page may be photocopied or reproduced with permission for student use.

Poetry Prompt 23

Art Show on the Horizon

Gorgeous sky scene, portrayed in layers—
the middle layer, redder than that stoplight,
is streaked with feathery, scarlet clouds
and glows almost supernaturally.
The bottom layer seems to portray mountains—
soft, gray smudges beneath the horizon's fiery crown.
And above, near the top—
a blanket of blue-gray seems to be lowering itself,
threatening to smother the fire below it.

Curved glass covers the breathtaking scene;
the frame is long and trapezoidal
with rounded edges;
The top of the picture is marred, however,
by a projecting mirror,
reflecting cars.

If I were standing in a gallery now,
instead of sitting in my car,
I might scoff at the picture,
insisting that it failed to be truly awesome.
After all, who ever heard of a sky that looked
so unrealistic?

Copyright ©2006 *Writing Success Through Poetry*, Susan L. Lipson. This page may be photocopied or reproduced with permission for student use.

For Discussion:

1. This poem is not about a painting, is it? What is it about?
2. What words in the second line give the first clue about the setting of the scene being described? What other clues in the second verse show you where the narrator is sitting to view this scene?
3. What is the author talking about in the lines: "curved glass covers the breathtaking scene," and "a projecting mirror, reflecting cars"?
4. The last verse uses *irony*—humor to poke fun at, or make a witty point about something; for example, this last verse makes a point about art appreciation and nature. Have you ever seen a natural view that looked so perfect it seemed fake?

Exercise: Write a five-sentence thematic paragraph to explain the relation of this poem's message to the well-known quotation, "Truth is stranger than fiction." Your opening lines could read something like this:

> Just as people often say, "Truth is stranger than fiction,"
> in relation to incredible true stories, the poem "Art Show
> on the Horizon" shows us how nature . . .

After concluding that topic sentence, continue the paragraph by referring to, and/or quoting from, "Art Show on the Horizon," to illustrate how nature's beauty can be underestimated, even called unrealistic, by those who have never taken the time to enrich themselves outside of a museum.

Extension: Trade paragraphs with a partner, or some other writer whom you respect. Edit for each other (for content, logical flow, power, and appropriateness). Then trade back, revise, and trade again, this time for proofreading. Proofread for misspellings, punctuation problems, grammar issues, and typos.

Further Extension A: Make a list of things in nature that seem too perfect to be real. Write about one of those items in either a prose piece or a poem to illustrate the natural beauty, as well as a person reacting to that beauty with disbelief. Maybe your person could view the thing for the first time in his or her life. For example, a grandmother might gaze, open-mouthed, at a tall cactus when visiting her grandchildren in California for the first time from her home state of Michigan.

Further Extension B: Look up the word *awesome*. Write down its definitions, but not the one labeled *slang*. The slang usage has threatened the extinction of this very powerful word. Next to the definitions you record, please write, "Awesome is not a synonym for cool." Finally, write a brief description of something that truly is awesome, and title it "Awed by _____."

Copyright ©2006 *Writing Success Through Poetry*, Susan L. Lipson. This page may be photocopied or reproduced with permission for student use.

Poetry Prompt 24

Night Time Visitor

My muse,
She visits me at night,
When most views dim,
But stars shine bright;
When thoughts flow forth
Like water poured,

The sparkling drops
In vessels stored,
As others rise into the sky,
Evaporating with a sigh
From she who has no name,
From she who has a claim
On this medium, my mind.

For Discussion:

Both of the following companion poems also deal with muses, the fictional spirits that give inspiration to writers. Discuss the poems' very different tones, structures, rhythms, and word choices. Read them each aloud.

Copyright ©2006 *Writing Success Through Poetry*, Susan L. Lipson. This page may be photocopied or reproduced with permission for student use.

Poetry Prompt 24, continued

To My New Muse

Hello Joy!
You're one fine muse!
Thanks for answering my ad so quickly.
I needed a replacement
for your half-sister, Sorrow.
It seems she's on vacation.
Let's hope she takes her time.

For Discussion:

1. When you write poems, which inspires you more often: sorrow or joy?
2. How does a sorrowful poem differ sometimes in structure from a joyful, or humorous poem?
3. Why does this poem call sorrow the "half-sister" of joy?

Copyright ©2006 *Writing Success Through Poetry*, Susan L. Lipson. This page may be photocopied or reproduced with permission for student use.

Poetry Prompt 24, continued

The Harvest

A poet has a field forever growing,
A field forever growing in her mind;
And sometimes she may bend to pick a sample,
A sample that has not yet reached its prime.
The sprouts curl up and shrink back from her fingers,
And though the poet tries to coax them, "Stay!"
She mustn't reach to grasp them, for they'll wither,
And all their seeds will fly away . . . away.

For Discussion:

1. Have you ever tried, like the poet in "The Harvest," to make a piece of writing work, knowing that it sounded forced, awkward, and certainly not ready for print?
2. How do you know when you are writing your strongest work? How does the process feel?
3. What is the "sample" in the poem?

Exercise: Write a poetic note to your own muse. What emotion best represents yours? Name her accordingly. Has she inspired you lately, or has she seemed to abandon you? Perhaps she won't leave you alone during homework, distracting you with other creative ideas unrelated to school. Show what kinds of inspiration you feel, or wish you would feel. Show your appreciation or frustration with your muse.

Extension: Trade muse pieces with a partner, if possible. Edit for each other; remember, no rewriting, only making suggestions. After receiving your critique, decide which of your partner's comments make sense to you and seem necessary. Then revise based on your decisions.

Further Extension A: If you could pick a famous writer to serve as your personal muse, to sit on your shoulder and whisper in your ear as you write, whom would you choose, and why? What quality does this writer have that you would like to develop? Write a short scene in which

Copyright ©2006 *Writing Success Through Poetry,* Susan L. Lipson. This page may be photocopied or reproduced with permission for student use.

Poetry Prompt 24, continued

you, frustrated by writer's block, benefit from a surprise visit with your famous writer muse. Show the answers to the above questions via the scene between an aspiring author and the mentor serving as his or her muse. If possible, quote from some of your favorite author's works.

Further Extension B: Experiment with similes. Note the line in "Night Time Visitor" that says, "When thoughts flow forth/Like water poured." That simile fits the idea of flowing thoughts; it is an apt simile. But, sometimes people force similes just because a teacher requires that they be included in a certain assignment, or because the writer hopes to sound more literary somehow. You can easily recognize a forced simile, though, because it may jar you, annoy you, or make you laugh with disdain. For example, to describe a tranquil sunset scene, you would not use this simile: The sunset looked like a bloody gash across the horizon. That description might work for a scene of impending horror, though!

You can use similes that jar the reader, however, if your intention is to jar. For instance, you could describe a person who lacks warmth in an ironic simile like this: Her hug left me feeling as warm as if I'd just hugged a snowman. Choose your words carefully, especially in similes.

Also, take note of this warning: Use similes sparingly—that means only a couple here and there. You will make your reader roll his or her eyes if your force similes into every other line to show off your skills with figurative language.

To practice writing similes, describe the following people in figurative terms that convey either how the person looks, sounds, or moves:

- a cold person (distant, unsociable);
- a nervous, uptight person (who cannot relax);
- a flaky, indecisive person (flighty, fickle, or capricious);
- an arrogant person (one who is overconfident, conceited, boastful, a show-off); and
- an insecure person (someone lacking a sense of self-worth, and sometimes, masquerading as an arrogant person to uplift social status).

Note: You could portray the last two people with the same description, showing the only difference as another character's reaction to their action. Have you ever noticed how the arrogant person usually needs to show off to make him- or herself feel more secure?

Copyright ©2006 *Writing Success Through Poetry*, Susan L. Lipson. This page may be photocopied or reproduced with permission for student use.

Poetry Prompt 25

Revision

My soles stride
through sunset-colored,
discarded paper balls,
crumpled and strewn about
by the ever creative Author of the seasons,
whose drafts grow in piles
that crunch beneath my heavy boots,
while the cold wind
leafs through the changes.
I kick a small pile upward, for fun,
and watch the fallen rise again,
only to flutter to the ground
and onto my feet,
as though to challenge me
to kick them around again.
The Author's metaphors of passing time
form tiny, swirling tornadoes,
crackling as they land
on dormant soil
to enrich it for the next season.
Thus, Mother Nature perfects her work.

Copyright ©2006 *Writing Success Through Poetry*, Susan L. Lipson. This page may be photocopied or reproduced with permission for student use.

Poetry Prompt 25, continued

For Discussion:

1. How is Mother Nature, author of the seasons, like an author of poetry or prose?
2. What are the "discarded paper balls," later called "metaphors of passing time"? (Hint: like time, they leave quickly.)
3. Why is fall a good time of year to compare to the revision process of writing? (Hint: What does fall have to do with future growth?)
4. What does *dormant* mean? How is *dormant* different than *dead*? How is the revision phase of writing similar to the dormant trees in fall?

Exercise: Choose your three favorite pieces from the collection of writings that you have created with this book. Choose the most developed draft of each piece. Reread and revise further or expand the work according to the editing guidelines in Appendix A. Even final drafts can improve with further changes.

Extension: Now compare the very first drafts with the newly revised versions in terms of description, action, dialogue, and mood, order, and matter (D.A.D. and M.O.M. elements). Take notes about the improvements in each area, for each work. Your best chance for growth as a writer—indeed, as a person, for that matter—is to master the art of introspection (self-examination and reflection).

Further Extension: Write an essay that proves that you have grown as a writer (your thesis will be an assertion about your obvious progress). Cite specific examples from your own first drafts and final drafts that illustrate your improvement. Consider this a final exam—more of a self-examination, actually—to call your attention to your growth as a writer.

Copyright ©2006 *Writing Success Through Poetry*, Susan L. Lipson. This page may be photocopied or reproduced with permission for student use.

Editing Checklist

Remember to double-space your written work for easier, clearer editing later. Complete the steps below, writing your brief comments (in numerical order) on a separate piece of paper so that you can re-use this checklist for everything you write or edit. If a number on the list—such as Draft One, No. 1—requires no answer or comment, simply write on your separate paper a check mark beside the step number to indicate your completion of that step. For those questions that do call for answers, please do not worry about using full sentences here; instead, think of this editing process as recording notes for yourself, a kind of self-made study guide to review later, prior to writing a new piece.

Draft One: First Level of Editing—Substance/Content

1. Listen to someone read the entire piece aloud to you, or read it to the author if you are editing for someone else. The reader should read slowly and with expression. If you have no one to read aloud for you, read your own work aloud, to allow yourself to hear your words outside of your own head.

2. Note your observations about the following issues:

   - Is the main idea clear or unclear?
   - Does the story or essay show a clear beginning, middle, and end, flowing along in a logical order?
   - Does the work move from point to point at a reasonable pace, maintaining a balance in the depth of each point or scene (versus rushing certain points or scenes without developing any depth)?
   - Does the work stay focused on its topic rather than veer off into unnecessary tangents, or side stories?
   - Do the word choices reflect the proper tone for the piece, and, in fiction, the proper voice for each character?
   - Do you enjoy hearing it aloud (without wincing over awkward-sounding parts)?

If you answered "no" to any of those questions, revise before continuing to the second level of editing, which follows.

Second Level of Editing—Style

1. Check for repeated adjectives and verbs, and delete those that add nothing to your piece. If the repeated words seem absolutely necessary for the reader's understanding, substitute words of the same meaning for the recurring words. Also, if any of your word choices strike you as not exactly

Copyright ©2006 *Writing Success Through Poetry*, Susan L. Lipson. This page may be photocopied or reproduced with permission for student use.

what you wished to convey, now is the time to find more powerful words. Use a thesaurus, if necessary.

2. Lightly circle all descriptive words and phrases.

   - Write "T" for telling over any description that tells, but doesn't show a word picture, such as opinion words that mean different things to different people (e.g., *ugly, scary, beautiful, awesome, old*) or words that can be imagined in more than one way (e.g., *sad, annoyed, shocked, excited, angry, kind, nice, big, little, smart*).
   - Replace every telling word with a more specific, colorful showing word or phrase. Use a thesaurus to help you.

3. Reread the changed sentences. Will your words paint a picture that stimulates more than just the visual sense in your reader? If not, look for a natural way to add a sound, smell, feeling, or taste to help the reader experience the scene, rather than simply observe it.

4. Have you included a *simile* or *metaphor* in any of your descriptions? Try to include at least one in your work, but no more than two in a paragraph.

5. Lightly underline all verbs and verb phrases. Immediately delete any of the following passive verbs (except when no alternative exists): *am, is, are, was, were, be, being, been, go, goes, went, do, does, did, say, says, said.*

6. Replace the passive verbs with active verbs that *show* an action, not just *tell* about it. If the passive verbs follow *there*—as in *there was, there is, there were,* and *there are*—delete there from the sentence, as well. Also, replace *said,* whenever possible, with a dialogue tag that shows how a character says his or her words (e.g., *whispered, shouted, snapped, cooed, barked*).

7. Look at the rest of the underlined verbs and verb phrases. Label "D" for dull over any vague words and replace them with more specific ones (e.g., *sprinted* instead of *ran,* or *snapped* instead of *said in a mean voice*).

8. Have you used any dialogue or quotations to show what someone says to illustrate your ideas or main points? Add either of these types of spoken words if possible. When writing nonfiction, remember to cite your source in parentheses after quoting other authors.

For Draft Two:

1. Recopy or retype the piece with the changes.
2. With your fresh-looking copy in hand, proofread for misspellings, punctuation problems, paragraph formatting errors, and grammatical difficulties. Correct the errors you have identified.

Copyright ©2006 *Writing Success Through Poetry*, Susan L. Lipson. This page may be photocopied or reproduced with permission for student use.

3. Ask someone who has more writing experience than you to read your second draft and proofread it for you. A fresh pair of eyes can make a significant difference at this stage.

4. Make any final changes based on your reader's suggestions— if you agree with him or her.

5. Carefully recopy or type the changes onto the document.

6. Reread the final draft. Write on a separate piece of paper the grade or evaluation that you would give your work based on the quality of your previous works and on a rubric founded upon the relative strength of each piece (see Writing Rubric in Appendix B).

7. Turn in your final draft for a teacher or peer's evaluation. Later, compare the reader's assessment to your own. If they differ a lot, be sure to discuss why with your reader.

8. File your work by date so that you can chronicle your progress as a writer. Review your work, from first to final draft stage. Learn from mistakes; they're tough, yet helpful teachers. Also, keep in mind that some critiques are matters of opinion, not fact. Make sure you agree with and accept the criticism before you make further changes in your work.

Writing Rubric

1	2	3	4	5	6
A weakly written, barely readable piece that merely tells without showing, using vague, forgettable word choices and making no use of the D.A.D. or M.O.M. techniques. A 1 exhibits a lack of knowledge of, or attention to, or knowledge of, basic writing mechanics, with frequent errors in basic mechanics, also known as proof-reading issues, such as problems with spelling, punctuation, format, grammar, and unnecessary extra words.	A piece that uses one or two aspects of the D.A.D. and/or M.O.M. elements, but possesses little word power in its mostly nonspecific word choices. A 2 also shows numerous errors in basic mechanics, though not as many as a 1.	The piece shows a balance between its strengths and weaknesses, indicating the potential for a powerful revision. A 3 offers some memorable lines and uses at least three of the D.A.D. and/or M.O.M. elements.	A work in which the strengths overpower the weaknesses, and the weaknesses are limited to minor stylistic and/or proofreading issues to resolve, rather than substantive problems. D.A.D. and M.O.M. clearly influence a 4, even if the writer has not mastered the subtle use of those elements yet.	The writer has created a powerful, memorable work that clearly shows the writer's control of both the D.A.D. and M.O.M. skills by using specific, apt word choices and a strong, yet subtle style. A 5 needs no editing, only proofreading—for either very few misspellings, incorrect punctuation, or minor grammatical errors.	Vivid, memorable writing that employs the D.A.D. and M.O.M. models, painting a clear, logical, multisensory word picture or argument (in the case of an essay), without any mechanical errors. A 6 motivates the reader to reread the piece for enjoyment.

Copyright ©2006 Writing Success Through Poetry, Susan L. Lipson. This page may be photocopied or reproduced with permission for student use.

Basic Rules for Writing

1. The main purpose of writing is sharing—to share the images and ideas from your brain with your reader in the clearest, most vivid, and fewest possible words.

2. Word power is a matter of quality, not quantity; one well-chosen word can outshine a page of vague, superfluous lines.

3. Writing is a process, nurtured by meaningful feedback and time away from the work to gain a clearer perspective for true editing.

4. Editing must be a two-step process: First comes substantive editing, for matters of substance and style, and then comes proofreading for misspellings and errors in punctuation and grammar.

5. Hearing your work read aloud to a group may feel embarrassing at first, but once you get used to hearing applause and comments about your words, you gratefully accept the attention and often feel surprised at the impact you have made.

6. Hearing your work read aloud greatly benefits self-editing, enabling you to hear your work outside of your own head.

7. Painting vivid word pictures for your reader is easy if you use the D.A.D. technique to show, rather than tell what is happening.

8. All writing is creative, no matter what genre, and the key to maintaining the reader's interest is lively details.

9. No writing is *good* or *bad*, only *weak* or *strong* (which leaves room for growth).

10. Writers must establish their own current standards for their best work, and then modify their standards as their skills improve.

11. Signing or printing your name on a piece of writing (the byline) ought to signify your pride in that work. Only add your byline to words that make you proud.

12. "What is written without effort is read without pleasure" (Samuel Johnson, esteemed author).

Copyright ©2006 *Writing Success Through Poetry*, Susan L. Lipson. This page may be photocopied or reproduced with permission for student use.

D.A.D. and M.O.M. & the 6+1 Trait® Writing Standards

Many American schools today have established their standards for evaluation of student writings upon the highly acclaimed 6+1 Trait® model for writing assessment, developed by the Northwest Regional Educational Laboratory (NWREL), in Portland, OR. You may read more about the 6+1 Trait® Assessment Scoring Guide on-line (http://www.nwrel.org/assessment).

NWREL's model encompasses the following six traits regarding the substance of a written work, plus an additional trait regarding its appearance:

1. Ideas
2. Organization
3. Voice
4. Word choice
5. Sentence fluency
6. Conventions
   + 1. Presentation

Note how the D.A.D. and M.O.M. elements of writing correspond with, and reinforce, the above six substantive traits:

Description, Action, Dialogue   ⟶   Ideas, Word choice, Voice

Mood, Order, Matter   ⟶   Voice, Word choice, Organization, Sentence fluency, Conventions

Descriptions show specific ideas (Trait 1) via adjectives and figurative language. Such descriptive language maximizes the power of the author's word choices (Trait 4) by creating multisensory imagery to establish both ideas (Trait 1) and voice (Trait 3) in subtle, meaningful, memorable ways. For example, a simile can convey an idea, as well as an image, in this way: Trees swayed like mourners at a graveside against the gloomy sky. The descriptive word choices in that simile convey a solemn narrative voice (Trait 3).

Actions show ideas (Trait 1) via vivid verbs. Active word choices (Trait 4) affect the reader's involvement in a piece of writing. In fiction, the actions of characters interact with the narrative voice (Trait 3) to convey multidimensional personalities to the reader. Subtle use of actions, coupled with descriptions, sometimes lends as much to the voice of a piece as the dialogue does. Consider this example: "Well, hello, sweetie!" she exclaimed, stretching her lips across her clenched, perfect teeth, as though for an orthodontic exam—her version of a smile. The ironic tone of the narrative voice clearly comes through the description of the character's actions.

Copyright ©2006 *Writing Success Through Poetry*, Susan L. Lipson. This page may be photocopied or reproduced with permission for student use.

Dialogue, like action, shows ideas (Trait 1) via spoken words, and the specific word choices (Trait 4) show each speaker's point of view or voice (Trait 3). In nonfiction, dialogue corresponds to the quotations used, which represent words "spoken" by other writers. The characters or other authors who speak in a written work reveal ideas and move plots along by how they respond to other speakers.

Mood, the first element in the M.O.M. technique for writing, is closely related to voice (Trait 3) in that it refers to a tone set by specific word choices (Trait 4) and the particular organization (Trait 2) of those words. For example, to convey a mysterious mood, a writer may organize the revealing of details in sporadic, purposefully vague words that merely imply what will happen in the story, thereby keeping the reader begging for more.

Order, the second element of M.O.M., ties in with the trait of organization (Trait 2), not only of details and thoughts, but also of a work's guiding structure that controls the reader's perceptions of ideas. A story, for instance, may use an anachronistic order of events to enhance the reader's suspense, and the creation of such an order depends upon the trait of sentence fluency (Trait 5) for a natural-sounding flow of ideas. Similarly, the order used in an essay, in building an argument, relies on the organization (Trait 2) of the concrete details and commentary lines, as well as on sentence fluency (Trait 5) and conventions (Trait 6), for skillfully crafted transitions and varied and sophisticated sentence structures determine the cohesiveness, clarity, and power of the writer's position.

Matter, the final part of the M.O.M. mnemonic device, ties directly into each of the 6 Traits: first, the matter on the page must matter, which calls for specificity in word choices (Trait 4), organization (Trait 2), and relevant ideas (Trait 1). Superfluous words call for deletion, and each word must maintain a consistency in voice (Trait 3), and contribute to sentence fluency (Trait 5). Writers convey matter via their skills in the use of conventions (Trait 6)—without which the matter on the paper does not really matter, for the reader can easily confuse the meaning of a work when the writing lacks clarity.

Thus, by consciously practicing the D.A.D. and M.O.M. techniques while writing, students will naturally develop the six substantive traits that serve as today's standards for writing evaluation.

The additional single trait identified by NWREL, presentation (+1), added by educators for the clever purpose of isolating the influence of a work's superficial appearance on a teacher's scoring of that work, aptly illustrates the assertion in the beginning of this book that teachers must practice and teach two separate levels of editing. First, students and teachers must focus on matter, and finally, on artistic presentation. Again, to quote Shakespeare: "More matter, less art."

Copyright ©2006 *Writing Success Through Poetry*, Susan L. Lipson. This page may be photocopied or reproduced with permission for student use.

Essay Writing Guidelines

Format of a Basic, Five-Paragraph Essay: The Essay Sandwich—A Directed Drawing Experience

Visually picture the essay format as a toasted turkey, cheese, and tomato sandwich. On a blank sheet of paper, develop your own drawing of The Essay Sandwich according to the following description, and label each part (see Figure 1 for an example). When you have finished your "sandwich," and read the page accompanying it, you will present it aloud to someone else to ensure that you remember it.

First, draw a thick top slice of bread to represent the Introduction paragraph. In the center of that slice, write: "Paragraph One—Introduction." Shade the top of this Introduction slice to show it as toasted, and label that toasted layer with an arrow as follows: "Attention Getter—Crisp, Golden, Entices Readers to Bite." Below the toasted top, again with an arrow, label the middle of the bread: "Summary of Body—The Fiber Presenting the Main Points to Come." On the bottom of the upper slice of bread, draw a thick layer of mustard or ketchup to flavor the entire sandwich, thus representing the main argument of the essay, which you will label: "Thesis—The Condiment That Flavors the Entire Sandwich."

Next, draw a thick slice of turkey under the bread and label it in the center: "Paragraph Two—Meaty, Concrete Details Supported by Commentary." Directly below the turkey, draw a slice of cheese and label its center: "Paragraph Three—Blends With Meat, Adding More Flavorful Details and Commentary." Then draw a slice of tomato, labeled "Paragraph Four—Adds Zesty Flavor to the Cheese, More Concrete Details and Commentary." To the right side of these three paragraph layers, draw a bracket showing the connection between the turkey, cheese, and tomato, and label it: "The Body."

Under the Body, draw the bottom slice of bread, a bit broader than the Introduction slice, and label it "Paragraph Five—Conclusion" (broader than Introduction). Along the upper side of that bread, where it touches the tomato, shade a thin layer of extra mustard or ketchup and label it with an arrow to the right of the drawing: "Restatement of Thesis—Extra Dab of Condiment Rounds Out the Sandwich." Label the middle of that bread, using another arrow: "Review of Body—Discussion of What the Paper Teaches." Finally, shade the bottom of the sandwich to show the bread as toasted, and label that crispy layer: "Attention Keeper—Connected to Attention Getter, Leaves a Memorable Aftertaste."

Now, title your diagram: "The Essay as a Sandwich." Afterward, remember to present your diagram to someone else and explain it in your own words.

Copyright ©2006 *Writing Success Through Poetry*, Susan L. Lipson. This page may be photocopied or reproduced with permission for student use.

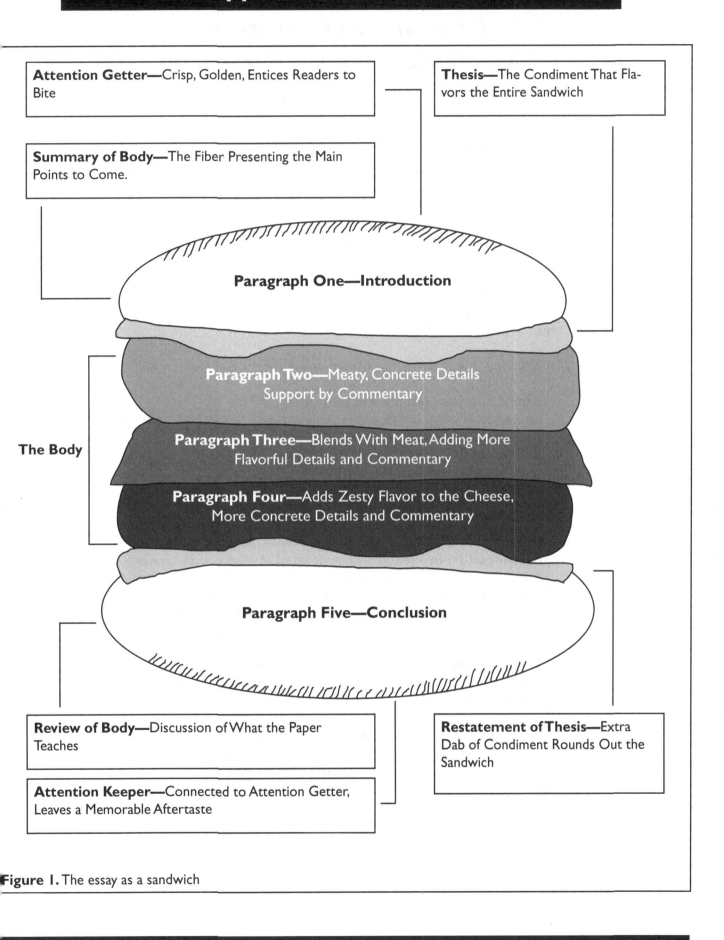

Attention Getter—Crisp, Golden, Entices Readers to Bite

Thesis—The Condiment That Flavors the Entire Sandwich

Summary of Body—The Fiber Presenting the Main Points to Come.

Paragraph One—Introduction

Paragraph Two—Meaty, Concrete Details Support by Commentary

The Body

Paragraph Three—Blends With Meat, Adding More Flavorful Details and Commentary

Paragraph Four—Adds Zesty Flavor to the Cheese, More Concrete Details and Commentary

Paragraph Five—Conclusion

Review of Body—Discussion of What the Paper Teaches

Restatement of Thesis—Extra Dab of Condiment Rounds Out the Sandwich

Attention Keeper—Connected to Attention Getter, Leaves a Memorable Aftertaste

Figure I. The essay as a sandwich

Copyright ©2006 *Writing Success Through Poetry*, Susan L. Lipson. This page may be photocopied or reproduced with permission for student use.

Response to Literature: Description of Each Paragraph in the Five-Paragraph Essay

Paragraph One—Introduction

Even though the thesis comes at the end of this paragraph, write it on a separate piece of scratch paper before any other sentence. Writing the thesis first will force you to focus on your main argument. If a sentence in your essay does not support the thesis in some way, remove it to keep your essay from wandering off track.

Once you've written the thesis, you can then build up around it, in essence, writing your Introduction backwards. The Introduction usually starts with more general ideas, and gets more specific along the way to the thesis. The Introduction should contain at least three sentences, as shown below:

Sentence 1: The Attention Getter, consisting of either:

- a quotation from the piece of literature;
- an anecdote (very short story) related to, or recounting part of, the piece of literature;
- an intriguing question raised by the piece of literature, possibly to be answered within the essay; or
- an informative or surprising statement (again, short and relevant).

Sentence 2: Summary of the Body—Points One, Two, and Three may appear either in one tightly constructed sentence or in separate sentences, if necessary. Use vivid words, but you may, in this case, tell more than show, since you will show examples in the body of the essay. Your points in a character analysis essay, for example, could cover:

- how the main character acts at the beginning of the story,
- how the main character changes in the middle of the story, and
- how the main character evolves by the end of the story.

Sentence 3: The Thesis should contain very specific words that define the argument to be proved by the essay, thus serving to outline and connect every idea to follow in the body. Often the thesis begins with words such as:

- Thus,
- Therefore,
- In sum,
- One can see that,

Copyright ©2006 *Writing Success Through Poetry*, Susan L. Lipson. This page may be photocopied or reproduced with permission for student use.

- Although,
- This story proves,
- This story demonstrates, and
- For this reason.

Paragraphs Two, Three, and Four—The Body

The five sentences in each of the body paragraphs feature specific examples, or concrete details, followed by commentary to illustrate and support the main points stated in the Introduction. Here's your chance to employ the "show, don't tell" rule of writing, and, remember, quotations from books make wonderful showing, supporting examples in literary essays. Maintain your focus on the thesis and choose concrete details that will not lead your essay into irrelevant wandering. After each detail or example, you should add at least two commentary sentences to enrich your reader's understanding.

Remember to craft *transitions*, bridges that connect each paragraph to the one before and/or after it. Repeating a word or idea from a preceding line works well, often with the help of transitional words such as:

- In addition to,
- Furthermore,
- Similarly,
- Conversely,
- Next,
- Also, and
- However.

The *Topic Sentence* states a general point or theme—although it should use specific, not vague, words—to set up the even more specific, illustrative sentence that follows it. Each topic sentence evolves from the main points mentioned in the introductory paragraph. In an essay that shows the change in one character over the course of a story, your topic sentence might begin: "At the beginning of the story" or "The story opens with" (for the other body paragraphs, you could use lines such as: "By the middle of the story" or "At the end of the story").

The *Concrete Detail* aims to illustrate the topic sentence with a very specific example. Detail helps you prove the point you wish to make in the paragraph. A concrete detail may be a quotation or a direct reference to the piece of literature stated in your own words (paraphrased). In a character analysis essay, pick quotations, or describe in your own words examples from the story, that show traits via actions and/or reactions of a character.

Please note: When using other authors' words or ideas, always show your source in parentheses after a quotation, like this: (Shake-

Copyright ©2006 *Writing Success Through Poetry*, Susan L. Lipson. This page may be photocopied or reproduced with permission for student use.

speare, p. 118). Include a bibliography at the end of an essay that uses multiple sources.

The *Commentary* helps support the concrete details. The commentary explains in your own words what the example shows. It should help the reader, who might not have read the book, story, or poem, understand what the author is showing. The commentary should also analyze why the concrete detail or example illustrates your thesis. Your commentary on each example will be at least two sentences, the first to explain the concrete detail, and the second to express your opinion about it. You might open with the words: "This example shows," "This quotation illustrates," or "The authors shows us this because."

The *Concluding Sentence* flows smoothly from your commentary sentences and adds a broader aspect to the main point of each body paragraph.

Paragraph Five—The Conclusion

Sentence 1—Restatement of Thesis: Leading with a transitional word or phrase to connect to the preceding paragraph, restate subtly and in fresh words your original thesis, in broader terms that apply either to the general public or to your reader. Make your reader come away from the essay with new thoughts to ponder or some lesson to recall. Do not use "I" in summarizing your ideas. You might open with one of the following:

- In sum;
- In conclusion; or
- Thus, we see that.

Sentence 2—Review of Body: Discuss how and/or what the story teaches us, rather than what it is about (do not summarize the piece again). You may want to write one sentence about how the events from beginning to end changed the character or how the character changed the events.

Sentence 3—Attention Keeper: Close with a statement as powerful as your Attention Getter. Make it an Attention Keeper, so that the essay does not just end, but rather, concludes—with impact. Readers appreciate circularity in an essay (when you return to a thought that opened the essay), making a neatly tied package. Thus, you might close with a final quotation, or refer back to the anecdote, statement, or question you might have used as your Attention Getter. The Attention Keeper eliminates any "so whats" from your reader's mind, making him or her think, "So *that's* why I needed to read this essay."

Copyright ©2006 *Writing Success Through Poetry*, Susan L. Lipson. This page may be photocopied or reproduced with permission for student use.

Sample Response to Literature Essay

by Elle Lipson, age 12

This model essay pertains to a short story, "The Stolen Party," by Liliana Heker. Each sentence can be labeled to correspond with the Essay Sandwich and its outline.

Stolen Dreams: A Response to Liliana Heker's
"The Stolen Party"

What we are in society sometimes matters more than *who* we are. In "The Stolen Party," Rosaura longs for a friendship with a girl outside her social class, and when the wealthy Luciana invites her to her birthday party, Rosaura thinks she has been asked as a friend until the end of the party, when she learns that she has been asked to come as a maid, like her mother. Thus, Rosaura changes through her realization of her lower position in the social classes.

At the beginning of the story, Rosaura has no sense of her lower status and actually feels confident about attending Luciana's party. When her mother questions her desire to attend the party of a girl who could never be her friend, Rosaura declares, "I'm going because I've been invited," and later, she walks "into the party with a firm step" (Heker, p. 2) These quotations show that Rosaura does not fear how the "other guests" might treat her. She foolishly believes that she has been invited as a friend. Rosaura is eager to fit in among the wealthy guests, and she won't let her mother's pessimistic, yet realistic, viewpoint stop her from participating in the party.

By the middle of the story, we see Rosaura as an active, enthusiastic participant in the party activities. For instance, "Rosaura won the sack race, and nobody managed to catch her when they played tag. When they split into two teams to play charades, all the boys wanted her for their side" (Heker, p. 3). Rosaura feels so enthusiastic because she thinks she is popular among most of the guests, and she is having a great time. When asked to help serve food, she assumes that she is simply the most helpful of the guests and a favorite of Luciana's mother. Rosaura, having decided to enjoy this birthday party, overlooks the reality she only comes to face it in the end.

At the end of the story, she feels furious at being treated like the lower-class person she realizes she is. Instead of Senora Ines giving her a party favor, as she gave to all of the other children, "In her hand appeared two bills . . . Rosaura felt her arms stiffen, stick close to her body . . . Rosaura's eyes had a cold, clear look . . ." (Heker, p. 4). Rosaura's stiffening and the coldness in her eyes indicate her sudden realization that she has never been Luciana's friend, only the daughter of the maid. Rosaura feels crushed, as well as furious, because the friendship with Luciana had become like a fantasy to her, an escape from her less exciting life. The end of her fantasy

Copyright ©2006 *Writing Success Through Poetry*, Susan L. Lipson. This page may be photocopied or reproduced with permission for student use.

shows Rosaura that the people in Luciana's world do not look at her as a person, but as a member of a lower social class.

Rosaura learns that differences in social classes affect the way some people think of her. After recognizing at the party that her social position prevented any real friendship with Luciana, she also realizes that she must redefine her idea of "friendship" as a relationship not based on social status. Therefore, we learn with Rosaura that people are people, with dreams and hopes like ours, regardless of any differences in social class.

Copyright ©2006 *Writing Success Through Poetry*, Susan L. Lipson. This page may be photocopied or reproduced with permission for student use.

Writing Skills Index

A list of specific writing skills covered in the exercises and extensions in the book appears below. The title of each poetry prompt that addresses the skill, along with the poetry prompt number in parentheses, is included.

About the Author

Susan L. Lipson, a published poet and children's novelist, has shared her passion for writing with students and teachers in the San Diego area since 1996. Susan works as a private writing coach, a guest instructor in schools, a consultant to teachers, a summer writing camp director, and a GATE writing program instructor. A former full-time editor and freelance writer, Lipson still edits occasionally, in addition to writing fiction, poetry, and songs. Her first children's novel, *Knock on Wood* (2000), launched her busy teaching career, as a result of a subsequent book tour through local bookstores and school assemblies. Poetry—Lipson's greatest literary love—forms the basis for many of her writing lessons, and files of her own poetry prompts have evolved into this book. Lipson lives in Poway, CA, with her husband and three children (ages 15, 14, and 12), and two dogs.

Printed in the United States
by Baker & Taylor Publisher Services